The Secrets of
PRACTICAL
MARKETING
FOR
SMALL
BUSINESS

Other books by Herman R. Holtz:

Government Contracts:
Proposalmanship and Winning Strategies

The $100 Billion Market:
How to Do Business With the U.S. Government

Profit From Your Money-Making Ideas

The Winning Proposal:
How to Write It (with Terry Schmidt)

Directory of Federal Purchasing Offices

Profit-Line Management

The Secrets of PRACTICAL MARKETING FOR SMALL BUSINESS

Herman R. Holtz

PRENTICE
HALL
PRESS

New York   London   Toronto   Sydney   Tokyo   Singapore

Published in 1986 by Prentice Hall Press
A Division of Simon & Schuster, Inc
15 Columbus Circle
New York, NY 10023

Originally published by Prentice-Hall, Inc.

PRENTICE HALL PRESS is a trademark of Simon & Schuster, Inc.

Library of Congress Cataloging-in-Publication Data

Holtz, Herman.
The secrets of practical marketing for small business,
Bibliography: p.
Includes index.
1. Marketing.   2. Small business.   I. Title.

HF5415.H7499   1982   658.8   82-9016
ISBN 0-13-798215-1 (pbk.)   AACR2

Manufactured in the United States of America

16   15   14   13   12   11   10   9   8

To Max and Reeva Goldberg for more than I can ever repay

Contents

Preface

It's a rare individual who doesn't see his or her own role as the most vital one in an enterprise, whether it's a role as a mother, breadwinner, corporate president, comptroller, or maintenance engineer. Each is convinced that the enterprise would grind to a halt without his or her own contribution and hard work.

In business, as in life, all roles are important; some are indeed critical to success. In the small enterprise, where the founder is in direct charge of everything and may even wear a number of hats, an ambivalence is inevitable. He or she is obviously the most critically important person in the organization, but in which role?

This is not a trivial matter. The enterprise may rise or fall on the founder's decision as to where he or she must devote the most time and attention, or which function to turn over to a hired manager and which to oversee personally.

As a businessman I must confess that I am prejudiced in the conviction that of all business functions, none is more important than that of marketing and sales. Enough success in this area can overcome most other problems, such as undercapitalization, poor cash flow, inventory control, accounting, and others. But without success in the marketplace, the greatest success in these other vital functions will not save the enterprise. The very identity of an enterprise as a business presumes that there are customers for whatever goods or services the enterprise offers. Clearly, it's not a business unless it has customers.

Peter Drucker, a widely accepted authority and best-selling author on the subject of business management, has said that the purpose of business is to create customers. And there is no doubt that Maurice L. Strauss, the "Moe" of the famous Pep Boys auto-stores chain "Manny,

Moe, and Jack," had the same thought in mind when he said, "Business is first. Worry about yourself second." Or that Ray Kroc, founder of the huge McDonald's hamburger success, was so motivated when he insisted on rigid standards of cleanliness, comfort, and uniformly high quality of food preparation. A multitude of success stories provide a mountain of evidence that not only is the purpose of business to create customers, but only with customers is there a business at all—only with customers in sufficient quantity, that is.

If a business is concerned primarily with creating customers, that function known as marketing is concerned primarily with *how* to create customers. But when A = B and B = C, A = C. Therefore, marketing and business are virtually synonymous. That is, if Business = Customers and Marketing = Customers, Business = Marketing.

Note that I use the term *marketing*, rather than *sales*. This is not literary choice nor semantics; it is deliberate and it is very much at the heart of the matter. There is a vast difference between the two functions. To put it more accurately, the sales effort is part of marketing. To pin the distinction down a bit more, even at the risk of oversimplification, *sales* is the function of getting orders, while *marketing* is the function of determining what kinds of orders to get, where and how to pursue them, how to appeal to prospects and motivate them to buy, advertising, and all the other things that must be done before a salesperson can be handed a sales portfolio and instructed to go forth and bring back orders (even for businesses that do not literally employ persons in the sales function).

If this suggests that marketing involves virtually all other aspects and functions of an enterprise, it is not accidental: Marketing, as a function, does stem from all other activities in the company—what to sell, how to make it, how to price it, how to advertise, where to meet the prospects, when and how to improve or otherwise change the service or product, how to package it, how to compete, how much to budget, and myriad other details.

In short, you cannot arbitrarily decide that you will force your offerings on the public and force them to accept these offerings by the power of your sales and advertising alone. The business boneyards are littered with the corpses of enterprises founded and conducted on that approach to marketing. You cannot simply guess at what will find acceptance, either: Who would have expected to be able to sell beach pebbles and a small brochure for four dollars (Pet Rocks), and who would have predicted that such giant corporations as RCA and GE would be failures in the computer business? Or that the mighty Chrysler Corporation would be forced to the brink of bankruptcy, with its salvation still far from certain? Or that W. T. Grant would collapse? The financial experts can find all kinds of explanations for these failures, but they are second causes; the first cause, in each case, is a failure of marketing: The consumers did not buy what the companies offered, although they did buy the same products and services from competitors. In each instance, sales efforts continued as before, even at an accelerated pace, but marketing had failed to gauge the market correctly.

Markets change because customers' motivations change in response to a variety of factors. That is, the *basic* wants do not change—customers still want home entertainment, for example—but they respond eagerly to better means for satisfying those basic wants: The ready acceptance of TV has been followed by a ready acceptance of games to be played on home TV sets, and videotape recorders and players are proliferating among those who can afford them. And with the wide variety of TV games now available, it would be pretty difficult to sell those early models, with their relatively primitive games.

So marketing is not a function you perform once, but rather a function that must be carried on continually, sensing all changes and responding properly to them.

Usually, the large corporation can well afford to hire staffs of marketing and sales experts (although some of the examples cited here suggest that they could not afford those "experts" who proved to be not so expert after all). The small company cannot afford this luxury, nor can it afford the luxury of making costly mistakes. At best, the small company has a limited staff capability in marketing functions, and frequently it is the owner-founder who must shoulder the principal burden for these functions. And even if the proprietor has some staff people in marketing, the proprietor—usually the chief executive officer, even in medium-sized companies—is the final judge of what is done in the name of marketing. Ergo, my conviction that of all the hats the small entrepreneur must wear, none is more deserving of time and attention than that labeled "Marketing/Sales Manager."

What we will examine in these pages, therefore, is the entire business situation for a wide variety of business enterprises, representing the entire spectrum of small enterprises in all their plans, concepts, and functions, for that is what marketing is. We will not dwell on economic theories or philosophies except, possibly, in passing, for this is to be a marketing "cookbook" for the small entrepreneur—how-to-do-it instructions and procedures, a do-it-yourself manual for the entrepreneur as marketer, with as many money-saving tips as the author knows of, many of which make possible marketing activities the small entrepreneur otherwise could not afford. You will learn, for example, how to use your advertising dollar most fruitfully and even how to get free advertising, how to use the media to your advantage, how to set up dealer networks or sales agents at no investment cost, how to write persuasive sales and advertising copy, and dozens of other "recipes" the small entrepreneur needs to set a full table of sales and success.

Herman Holtz
Wheaton, Maryland

1

What Is
a Business?

*Some people build their hobbies into businesses.
And others run their businesses as though they
were hobbies.*

A vice-president to whom I reported in one corporation which employed me years ago was fond of stating flatly that if we could not predict with reasonable accuracy what kind of business we would do in the coming year—what we would sell, in what volume, and to which customers—we did not have a business. Even if we did more business in the coming year than we had forecast, if we did it along lines far different from those projected, that was luck, he insisted, not control. And without reasonable control, how can you call it a business?

I was compelled to agree with him because I had said almost the same thing myself, on another occasion. I had joined a company as editorial director of a group whose mission was to create training programs in a format known as programmed instruction of the branching variety. When I joined this company, I had been advised by its president that writers who could become proficient at producing the company's specialized product were hard to find. Even thoroughly experienced and capable writers often proved incapable of mastering this special technique, I was told.

I could not accept that. If, in fact, our success in producing what we sold depended on our ability to find those occasional geniuses, we really had no control at all and, hence, no business. How could we possibly contract to deliver something without a certainty that we could recruit the staff required to produce that something?

As it turned out, the company president was wrong, and I found it possible to train and direct competent writers in producing what we needed. Had I been unable to do that I would have felt compelled to

1

counsel the firm to close its doors and forget about the business they were in.

In both cases we're talking about marketing—knowing what we're going to sell, to whom, in what quantity, and how/where to get what is sold. Sales concerns itself only with getting those orders, with making customers out of prospects. But marketing must do everything else that enables sales to get those orders and convert those prospects into customers.

WHAT ARE THE BASIC INGREDIENTS?

We have been talking about *functions:* buying or creating things to sell, identifying markets and prospects, forecasting and setting targets, and making sales. But what are the basic *ingredients* that must be present to qualify an enterprise as a business?

Regardless of what a dictionary or legal definition may be, for our purposes let us agree that a business is an enterprise that one enters into for the express purpose of drawing therefrom a living and, hopefully, a profit. Ergo, if the enterprise does not furnish its owner a living, is it still a business? Yes and no. It is still a business while the owner is operating it in the hopes that as it becomes established it will, indeed, begin to furnish an adequate living to its owner and other employees, if any. Should the enterprise never become viable as a source of living wages to its owner and other employees, the question is answered by the fact of the enterprise being necessarily abandoned.

For the enterprise to pay rent, heat, light, telephone, advertising, wages, and acquisition costs of goods or services sold, obviously it must sell those goods and/or services at a sum greater than the acquisition cost. And, of course, the difference between the acquisition cost and the selling price—the gross profit, that is—must be great enough to pay for all those other items just mentioned.

The logical consequence of this chain of reasoning is simple enough: Whatever the enterprise offers for sale—goods, services, or both—must be of enough value to enough prospects to induce them to buy at a profit great enough for the enterprise to meet all its expenses, at the minimum. (But it isn't much of a business if there is not at least a bit of profit left over after all expenses are met.)

So, to establish a business you must have something of value to sell, and the value must be great enough to defray all costs and enable you to make a living out of what's left.

Elementary? Indeed it is. Yet a surprising number of beginning entrepreneurs show evidence of not understanding even these elementary facts. In any case, it is necessary to make the point if the chain of logic to be presented is to be complete. For a business—any business—is necessarily based upon the concept of *value*, but value is not an absolute.

WHAT IS VALUE?

There is a discipline known as value engineering, also known as value analysis, value management, and a few other names. The specialists who practice this profession have always had a bit of difficulty in defining value. One problem is that value varies with the view of the individual. Attend any auction sale and you will soon agree, as you listen to the amounts different bidders are willing to pay for a given item. But value also varies with circumstances: Many items appreciate sharply in value when they are in short supply or when the demand for the item suddenly accelerates, for whatever reason. Value may vary according to a number of other factors, such as a change in some related cost (e.g., transportation and shipping costs).

At the same time, the definition of value as established by a value engineer is not quite the same thing as the definition of value as established by a merchant or trader. The value engineer is trying to establish a value for the purpose of setting a target—the goal is to reduce cost without affecting quality or utility, hence a need for value as an absolute quantity—at least for the time during which the value analysis is being carried out; and value engineering tends to be concerned more with supply-side economics than with demand- or consumer-side economics.

The marketer, whether he is a merchant or manufacturer, is necessarily concerned primarily with consumer economics because the principal concern and eventual goal of marketing is inevitably sales. The marketer must be concerned with value on a continual basis—not only with current value, but with trends in value, such as probable increases and decreases in value. One thing the marketer may be sure of is that value is never a constant over any significant period of time—everything offered for sale, whether goods or service, changes in value with time. Some items, such as commodities traded on stock exchanges, fluctuate constantly, although the overall trend for some years has been that all commodities tend to rise in price and, presumably, in value. Still, there are some items that buck the overall trend—sometimes for the short term, sometimes for the long term. And many of the items that decline in value will never resume their original values. Buggy whips and horseshoes are not likely ever to be greatly in demand again. Their decline is due to obsolescence, of course. But many electronic items have declined steadily in value—pocket calculators are a good example. They have declined because mass production has cut manufacturing costs, but competition and overproduction have been factors, too. And while this has been taking place, slide rules have become museum pieces, and are virtually worthless in today's marketplace.

Value, then, is simply what a customer is willing to pay for some item, goods or service, at any given time. If the majority of prospects refuse to pay the price a seller asks, obviously they do not agree with the seller's estimate of the value. The true value must necessarily be whatever the customers will pay; ergo, it is the customers who determine what the value is.

Customers do not make this determination in a vacuum. Many factors are involved. Customers are usually aware of what the general market is for the item—that is, what other sellers are asking for a similar item *or what they think is a similar item*. Once again we are running into the customers' perceptions; they are all-important.

ARE VALUE AND PRICE THE SAME THING?

If we use our terms carelessly enough, we can easily become confused and begin to believe that sellers dictate value by setting prices. That would mean, if it were true, that price and value mean the same thing. But we know that is not true. Price equals value only when and if the buyers are generally willing to pay the price.

Price is determined by certain specific factors. The first is what the item being offered costs the seller, whether it is purchase cost or manufacturing cost. A second factor is what it costs to sell the item, and that includes rent and other overhead involved in offering, selling, and delivering the item. A third factor is profit, and most sellers have some firm minimum profit they demand—except in certain special circumstances, when they will sell at cost or even below cost, because circumstances make it necessary.

Profit margins are arbitrary, according to the seller's ideas of what is the proper or necessary margin. One seller offers a television receiver at $449.95, while a competitor offers the identical item at $419.95. Why the difference? It may be due to any of several factors:

Differences in operating costs, meaning lower or higher "selling costs."
Differences in buying power, meaning lower or higher acquisition costs.
Differences in profit margin.

Special factors, such as a need for ready cash or a desire to unload slow-moving merchandise, or even to create a "leader" item to bring traffic into the store, in the hope of selling other merchandise.

If you were to shop a dozen establishments offering that same television receiver, you would probably find it offered at as many as six or perhaps even a dozen different prices. Theoretically, only the seller offering the item at the lowest price ought to do any business with it. That is, one might expect all buyers to flock to that seller offering the lowest price. Yet, in fact, that seller might be doing least well, and the highest-priced seller might be selling the greatest number of receivers.

There are many reasons why this might be so. Studying those reasons and understanding them is one major reason for this book. Running a business successfully entails solving many problems, none of which is more important than marketing. The first requirement is to persuade the buying public—whoever they may be—to *accept* your offers, to buy from you, at your prices. That means to convince a large enough proportion of your prospective buyers that you are offering a good enough value to win their patronage.

DOES GOOD VALUE MEAN LOW PRICE?

There are some business people who are easily confused between value and price, and they attempt to confuse their prospective customers in the same way by claiming to offer extraordinary values, when they really mean that they have cut prices. This particular type of offer works with a certain class of customer who is unable to see anything beyond the price tag—if the seller manages to convince these buyers that the prices advertised are indeed low ones. But there are other buyers who are not especially impressed by claimed or even actual low prices because they want also, as part of what they buy, to obtain service, dependability, convenience, and other things that are part of value, as these buyers perceive it.

Once again, value depends on the customers' perceptions, and the customers are almost continually and infinitely variable, of course— although before long we shall establish certain defined classes of customers in order to have some basis for planning marketing strategies.

UNDERSTANDING YOUR BUSINESS

One absolute essential for successful marketing is to understand what business you are in. Shockingly, a great many business people fail to understand their businesses. They think they do understand their own businesses, but their marketing failures—and, unfortunately, in many cases the general failure of their businesses—demonstrate otherwise.

The problem is that most business people attempt to analyze and understand their businesses from their own viewpoints—what their enterprises represent to *them.* What they should be doing is analyzing their enterprises from the viewpoints of their customers to find out what the enterprises mean to those who patronize them. Whereas many—probably most—business owners are keenly aware of what they wish to sell, they are not aware of what the customers wish to buy and what the customers are, in fact, buying. Perhaps the operators of Amtrak sell me a seat on a Metroliner train, but I *buy* the convenience of being delivered from Washington, DC, to midtown Manhattan rather than to remote LaGuardia Airport. I buy the convenience of walking to my New York City destination from Pennsylvania Station rather than struggling with cabs or buses to get from the airport to the city. And I also buy greater convenience on this end of the Metroliner trip, too, avoiding the problems of getting to National Airport in Washington's Virginia suburbs and fighting my way to the departure gate. If Amtrak marketing people understood *all* the reasons people use the train in preference to the airplane, they would advertise and sell seats more effectively.

In short, is Amtrak in the passenger-train business or is it in the business of delivering passengers most conveniently to their destinations? Is the distinction an important one? Yes, and for more than one reason. The obvious reason the distinction is important is that the marketer who understands why a customer buys whatever the organization sells is in a far better position to prepare marketing and sales campaigns. But the matter goes beyond that, and here we again must distinguish between sales and marketing: Knowing what motivates customers to buy tells the executive what to offer—how to improve whatever the offering is and so make it even more appealing to the prospects.

In the case of Amtrak's Metroliner to New York City, it is important to find out how many passengers ride the train because they prefer the convenience of being delivered to midtown New York. If that investigation reveals that a large enough percentage of passengers are motivated primarily by this consideration (rather than price or fear of flying), Amtrak might burn a bit of midnight oil pondering ways to provide even more convenience to Amtrak Metroliner passengers, and induce even more prospects to become Metroliner passengers. How to sell what you have to offer is only a part of marketing; how to make your offer more attractive or how to modify your offer so as to make it more attractive is also a part of marketing, a part too often overlooked by marketers who fail to distinguish between sales and marketing.

Understanding what business you're in, then, is nothing more nor less than understanding what your customers buy from you. And to understand that, you must recognize that no one really buys *things*; they buy what the things *do* for them. In the case of the Metroliner, they buy convenient delivery to midtown New York, although some may be buying a less costly form of transportation or avoidance of the fear of flying, or even the leisure to read undisturbed for several hours. Meanwhile, others are flying, buying faster transportation, and so forth.

You can easily perceive that advertising professionals tend to grasp this concept by analyzing advertisements and TV commercials. Like the highly effective pitchmen of old, they concentrate not on the superior quality of the product, but on the superior results one gets from using the product—on what the product does. Never mind the superior ingredients in Blank's dishwasher detergent; keep your eye on the superior sparkle of dishes and glassware washed with Blank's detergent, for this is what the prospect is really buying. In the final analysis, the user really doesn't care whether your detergent is biodegradable or not, whether it contains phosphates, whether the ingredients are "pure," or any other logical reason for claiming superiority of product. The customer wants superiority of result, not superiority of product.

You might well ask, then why do many advertisers expend a great deal of effort—not to mention money—trying to prove that their products are superior to those of competitors? Ultimately, we'll address that question and discuss why we must "prove" our claims and how we do so. But for the moment we are more concerned with understanding the basic motivations of our customers.

CHANGE AND WHAT IT MEANS IN BUSINESS

Nothing lasts forever. Death and taxes are not the only things we can always be sure of. We may count on change, also. Change is inevitable, and the entrepreneur is well advised to consider the inevitability of change and how it will affect the entrepreneur's business. Everything becomes obsolescent eventually, and while some things last for many years, others become obsolescent in a matter of weeks.

One example of fairly recent vintage is the Hula Hoop toy. Originating in Australia, although its invention is often credited to Arthur "Spud" Melin, president of Wham-O, the hoop toy came here in 1958. Originally it was made of rattan, which proved rather unsatisfactory. Only when Melin began to make the hoop of plastic did it become practical to produce it rapidly, in quantity, at modest cost. It didn't catch on immediately, but when it did, it went like wildfire. The peak of the demand lasted only a few weeks, however: It was definitely a short-lived fad. Despite the fact that hoops are still sold, a great many toy manufacturers got stuck with large quantities of hoops they produced a bit too late to cash in on the fad.

This is not an isolated case. Very much the same story may be told for the device that came to be known as a mood ring, for Pet Rocks, and for many other items. One does not know, when a new idea catches on, whether it will be around for many years or be moribund in a few months. In the case of the hoop toy, those who were able to turn the things out rapidly and get them to market immediately made a bit of money—several fortunes were made, reportedly—while those who were unable to move rapidly enough failed to cash in; some even were hurt financially.

However, a fad such as that of the hoop toy hardly has time to get settled in as an item of trade before it's all over, so probably it should not be even considered when we discuss change and obsolescence. More classic is the case of the buggy whip, which slow-to-change business people refused to abandon, even when there was overpowering evidence that horses and buggies were rapidly disappearing from the highways. Corporate graveyards are littered with the bones of entrepreneurs who refused to change. It is sad enough that many entrepreneurs lack the vision to gauge the possibilities of new products and new ideas, but it is even more tragic that many are unable to read the handwriting on the wall, no matter how boldly it spells out change and onrushing obsolescence.

A study of a few years ago turned up the not-too-surprising evidence that in general, those companies who plowed back substantial amounts of money in research were outperforming those who did not. Such companies are not only highly conscious of change and the inevitability of change, but they are actually instrumental in bringing change about.

Around 1960 a number of office copying machines were on the market. All were considerably less satisfying and convenient than users wished. Those using dry processes produced copies of poor quality, while those using other processes produced slightly better copies, but they were laborious and slow. The need for a better office copier was becoming more apparent every day, as the "information explosion" and the "paper explosion" proved to be realities. Still, the poor wretch who had invented a better copying method—in principle—was having a difficult time convincing anyone that he had something worth investigating seriously, much less worth investing money into. Fortunately for him and for millions of soon-to-be users, someone at a small company known as the Halide Corporation showed more vision than others had, and the seeds were planted which would sprout the Xerox Corporation, along with an entire new industry.

Probably it took no great vision to recognize the genuine need for a better office copier, and the fact that this was a permanent need, not a fad. The vision required here was to see that this new xerographic process was the answer to the problem, and would become the basis for a great company. The original equipment was a rather clumsy and costly affair that was no great improvement over existing machines, as far as speed and convenience were concerned. But it represented a definite improvement in copying quality, and the backers had enough foresight to see that faster, more convenient, and more efficient models would eventually be designed. The positive factors were that there was most definitely a hungry market for copying capabilities and that the market was almost universal—it would be hard to conceive of an industry or business which would not want (need) these machines. Couple to those factors the exclusive patents protecting this revolutionary breakthrough in the art of copying, and it was to be many years before anyone else could duplicate the attractive features of these original machines. But the manufacturer did not doze but maintained active R & D, and produced newer and better machines every year, even during the years when the competition could not come close to providing a machine that was competitive. The original Xerox machines were the only copiers capable of copying on plain paper during all those years that the machines had full patent protection on the basic invention; everyone else had to furnish special, treated paper, which was far less desirable than ordinary, untreated paper.

There is no doubt that when the Xerox product finally appeared in the marketplace, a great deal of money was lost by others who had invested large sums in developing their own copiers. In a very short time all those earlier machines became virtual museum pieces, and a number of years later, when the basic Xerox patents expired and other manufacturers converted from treated-paper copiers to plain-paper copiers, those treated-paper copiers became obsolete. (Some, priced at several thousand dollars originally, can now be had for as little as fifty dollars!) However, in this case the manufacturers were not taken unawares. They knew when the patents would expire and what that would mean to them, so they had ample time to prepare for the changeover.

Of course, many of the early Xerox machines are also obsolescent today, despite the fact that no one has ever improved on the basic xerographic method for copying, and the corporation has sold many of them at reduced prices. But despite the expiration of basic patents and the enormous proliferation of competitors producing plain-paper copiers, no one has been able to threaten the number-one position of the Xerox Corporation in the marketplace. If Peter Drucker's remark, "Business has only two basic functions—marketing and innovation," has any validity at all, that is amply demonstrated by this corporation, which constantly produces improved models, year after year, always in the forefront of innovative ideas.

SHORT-TERM VERSUS LONG-TERM NEEDS

We have taken a look at two extremes: the needs which are, in fact, fads because they are of such short duration, obsolete and over almost before they begin; and long-term, permanent needs being satisfied so well that competitors are unable to succeed beyond being "me too" runners-up, usually far behind the leader in sales volume. Does this mean that one should try hard to avoid being trapped by a short-term, faddish type of need?

The fact is that satisfying short-term needs is as sound a business idea as is satisfying long-term or permanent needs. But it is different and, in some ways, somewhat risky. Note, however, that for the fad or short-term need (the hoop toy; the mood ring) the investment was relatively small, while for the long-term need (the copying machine) the investment was much greater. In fact, a large investment would simply not be justified for marketing an item likely to be a fad; the risk is simply too great. One cannot be at all sure that a hoop or novelty ring is going to catch on. On the other hand, there was absolutely no doubt that a large market existed for a really efficient and convenient copier. The risk here was entirely one of gambling on the satisfactory engineering development of the machine.

Thus, *before* the enterprise is launched, it is a proper responsibility of the marketing function to judge the durability of the market, as well as its size, location, and other factors. We've used extreme cases here to illustrate the principles, but a great many cases are more difficult to judge than these. Who can tell whether a Nehru jacket will find favor with men (it didn't), or whether the time has passed for another season of miniskirts (it had), or whether women will agree to go to the opposite extreme and wear maxicoats (they wouldn't)? Obviously, the marketer is going to be right sometimes, wrong sometimes. Theoretically, it is necessary to be right only 51 percent of the time, but of course being wrong the first time may foreclose any possibility of having a second chance. Therefore, marketers use a variety of tools to reduce the hazards and improve the probability of being right. We'll discuss some of these as we proceed further.

This is not to say that a venture should not be undertaken if it is determined that the prospects are for a short-term market. In fact, many businesses are based on precisely this concept. The entrepreneur expects to market a product intensively, sell hard while the demand lasts, and get out rapidly when the demand begins to fall away. Such entrepreneurs are primarily—almost entirely—marketers: Their entire talent and all their efforts are focused on marketing, and they've no desire to build a business based on a product or line of products. Their chosen business is one of finding the item that can be heavily promoted, marketed successfully for some relatively short period—usually a matter of months—without great investment. When the peak of the sale is over—when demand has declined seriously and the profit margin has narrowed severely—the entrepreneur gets out, shuts down, and seeks the next item.

This describes how certain promoters function. Joe Cossman is one. Generally associated with mail order, Cossman does not restrict himself exclusively to mail order, but will sell his product of the moment—he rarely handles more than a single item at a given time—by other means also.

There are also enterprises that fall between the extremes. They usually have or are actively seeking one or more "hot" items which they hope will catch on during the current season, but they also have a growing line of items for which there is a steady demand, although not an enormous market. Toy manufacturers are one example of this, and book publishers another, with their back lists and the perennial hope of a best-seller or two each year.

Those who deal in only a single item at a time often express the opinion that it is not possible to market more than one item at a time and still do justice to the items. This, of course, reflects their chosen way of doing business, and is probably true enough for them. Other entrepreneurs feel differently about it, and believe that marketing an entire line of items at a given time is a far less risky approach to marketing. Both views are correct, of course, as long as they work for their advocates. Each entrepreneur must make his or her own decision as to which philosophy is best, the philosophy with which he or she is most comfortable and most successful. As they were fond of repeating at the Infantry School at Fort Benning, Georgia, "Whatever works is right."

2

Marketing Versus Sales: Is There a Difference?

The difference between marketing and selling is more than academic; it's at the heart of the entire strategy of the business.

EVEN LARGE CORPORATIONS DO NOT ALWAYS KNOW THE DIFFERENCE

The difference between marketing and sales is more than academic. It's a distinction that has proved to be the difference between survival and disaster for more than one enterprise. In a sense, the failure of any business is almost certainly a failure in marketing: A business that continues to maintain an adequate sales volume at an adequate margin of profit is almost certain to survive whatever problems it may have. On the other hand, sales volume below that acceptable minimum, is almost certain death, no matter how well-managed the business is in other respects.

Perhaps the classic case is that of the automation division of a large corporation whose business was the custom development of automated equipment for any customer who felt the need for automation. The company won a contract to design and build an automatic packer for high-quality chocolates. The product was a half-million-dollar machine, which was delivered and installed in the plant of the customer. Almost immediately, the sales force managed to get another order from another candy manufacturer for such a machine, and before assembly of that unit was well under way, the company won still another order.

So encouraged, the company decided to take advantage of the situation and build three extra models for stock, sure that they would find buyers for them readily. But many months later, the spare units stood gathering dust in a corner ot the factory. It seemed impossible to find buyers for them.

At this point, the company began to do their marketing—that is, they began to research the candy-manufacturing field, for the first time. To their horror, they discovered that there were only six candy companies in the entire world large enough to own and use such a machine. They had already saturated the market by selling to one half of it. This was not the cause of the company's demise, but illustrates why the company finally failed and had to be liquidated. So, in fact, they proved to be far better at sales than they were at marketing.

Putting it as simply as possible, sales is winning orders. Selling is part of marketing, in a way—the culmination of marketing, the *reason* for marketing. But sales owes much of its success—or lack of it—*to* marketing. Marketing is what identifies what is to be sold and to whom. Marketing decides how to package the product (or service), how to present it, how to advertise it, how to position it, to whom to offer it, how to reach the prospects, and just about everything else needed to finally place the offer in front of the prospect.

This is not to demean the function of sales forces or to suggest that sales is not itself a creative and critically important function. Without sales, marketing is meaningless: The entire purpose of marketing is to create those sales that are the very purpose of the business. But without marketing, sales may very well strike out blindly at the wrong targets, with the wrong offers, at the wrong times, and with the wrong presentations. So, while in many ways marketing and sales are all but indivisible —certainly they have a close relationship to each other—it is also necessary to distinguish the two functions from each other if we are to get a realistic look at that critical need to sell whatever it is that the business offers customers.

There are many classic cases of marketing failures that have led to the destruction of whole industries, as well as of individual corporations. The railroads are one classic case. Because they insisted on being in the railroad business instead of the transportation business, they began to lose passenger revenue to the rapidly growing airlines and freight revenue to the burgeoning trucking companies. Both competitors did a better job than the railroads were doing in terms of speed of delivery, as well as in other factors, such as convenience.

Companies whose existence depended on the railroads suffered also, of course. One was the U.S. Pressed Steel Car Company, founded in the late nineteenth century by the flamboyant Diamond Jim Brady. The company survived only because a manager with vision came along, renamed the company U.S. Industries, and took it out of the dying railroad-car business and into more modern lines. In fact, U.S. Industries is today a conglomerate of a large number of small companies, although the overall gross of the corporation is quite large.

The lesson is not learned by everyone. Among some more recent corporate casualties have been W. T. Grant, Korvette's, and Robert Hall, all retailers for whom astute marketing is or ought to be the *sine qua non* of its business existence. Who needs to be master of marketing more than a retailer?

The explanation of why once-successful companies such as these decline and fall into failure is sometimes management in general—for example, the Autotrain company overextended itself badly, made foolish investments, and swamped a once-profitable business with ruinous losses. But in most cases, the failure is one of marketing. Probably the most common situation or cause is the failure of the company's management to recognize that markets change and that marketing activities must keep pace and change with conditions. For example, Korvette's and Robert Hall were early entrants in the discount-chain field, attracting customers primarily with the lure of discounted prices. But the advantages they enjoyed because they got into the discount game early eventually were dissipated as discount competition grew. Nothing new happened in either of these two retail chains: They continued to market as always, apparently oblivious to what was happening around them, steadily losing their customer followings and doing nothing about it. The sales and marketing tactics that had once worked so well were no longer working, but still the companies pursued the same practices, evidently bewildered at the changes taking place in their markets and yet at a loss to grasp the changes or contemplate actions they ought to take in response to the changes. It's a lesson too many business organizations are unable to learn.

MARKETS ARE NEVER STATIC

One basic lesson every marketer must learn is that markets are never static. Some markets go on for many years with little or no change, while others are highly fluid, changing almost as you watch—but no market goes on forever without change. So, while a great many observers have noted that companies often fail to identify correctly the businesses they are in—with the railroads the outstanding horrible example most often cited—these same observers rarely explore the deeper meaning of that common failure. In fact, that failure is also a failure to recognize changes in the marketplace.

Using that classic case of the railroads as an example again, what the railroad magnates failed to observe and recognize was that they were in two markets: passenger travel and freight hauling. Both markets were changing because of inevitable technological advances: Airplanes were becoming bigger and safer, with regular service to more and more locations in the United States; and large automotive vehicles were being produced in large quantity, as a vast network of first-class major highways was being established swiftly.

Had the railroad operators done a proper job of evaluating these changes, they would have perceived a number of important factors which they should have considered:

- Air travel moved passengers swiftly and comfortably.
- Trucking lines delivered shipments more rapidly.
- Trucking lines offered great convenience, picking shipments up at the shipper's door and delivering directly to the consignee.
- Both classes of competitor, air lines and trucking companies, were highly competitive, offering all the inducements they could think of to win business away from the railroads.

Even these are only a few of the factors which should have alarmed the railroad owners and impelled them to take some defensive actions. A proper marketing analysis would have included at least the following initial steps:

- Analysis of the various *classes* of passengers and freight shippers.
- Development of marketing strategies for each class or type of customer so identified.

Obviously, while many passengers would switch to air travel because speed was essential (e.g., people traveling on business), there were others for whom speed was not of the essence (e.g., vacationers) and who *liked* train travel. For that class of passenger, the railroads could have and should have instituted services to make train travel even more attractive to those on leisurely schedules, or those for whom speed was not essential, but lower cost was.

Similar strategies should have been employed for freight, again finding those customers who could derive benefits from utilizing railroad facilities instead of trucking facilities, and going aggressively after this business.

Probably the railroads completely underestimated the threats posed by these upstart competitors, a not unusual failing. Successful business people often tend to become "fat, dumb, and happy" after enough years of success, and underestimate completely the drive and determination of hungry new competitors. More significantly, they stop studying their customers and their buying preferences. For that *is* the market—the customers' buying preferences, as shown by their buying practices.

A few years ago, for whatever reason, young people suddenly began to show a decided preference for jeans. Moreover, the shabbier and more faded the jeans, the more "in" they were. Suddenly, almost overnight, the poor relative of the clothing industry, formerly sold only in dry goods stores to farmers, ranchers, and laboring men, was being sold at premium prices in the finest clothing emporiums. Where a pair of good wool dress slacks might be offered at fifteen to twenty dollars, an adjacent rack carried denim jeans at twenty-five dollars or more!

There was no way to know whether this was a sudden fad that would run its course in a few months or a long-term trend. Consequently, clothing makers did not rush to convert their lines, and the bonanza fell into the laps of those old, established manufacturers of jeans and overalls. Once the tenacity of the market exhibited itself, others rushed into the breach and were soon offering designer jeans at even higher prices.

This latter is a somewhat curious development, which needs some analysis and evaluation. Whereas the heavy trend to jeans—particularly ragged and faded jeans—strongly suggested a trend away from style and fashion, the huge success of the many designer jeans demonstrates that jeans *are* a style trend, and that buyers of jeans *are* style and fashion conscious, when style and fashion trends are established. It seems obvious that astute marketers appreciated that behind the jeans movement lay that same reliable human need to be fashionable and in style. Smart marketing dictated marrying jeans to high fashion!

All of this falls in the realm of marketing, not sales. The most intensive sales activity will not help if the customers are not interested. Nehru jackets and maxicoats are pretty good evidence of that. The marketer cannot create the need—although many salespeople do speak of creating needs, and they evidently believe that they do. Let's have a look at what they are talking about by examining more closely what *need* means.

WANTS AND NEEDS

In an earlier time, the term *want* meant to be without, to lack, as in "the want of a nail." Today the word is commonly used to mean *desire*.

The word *need* also has more than one shade of meaning, according to who is using it and how. In one usage it means that one cannot do without something, as in, "I *need* a car." As sales and marketing people use the word, however, it refers to anything an individual wants (as in *desire*) or can be induced to want, whether the "need" means "can't do without" or "would like to have." In our case, we shall use the word in that sense, too. Whether we say "want," "need," or some other synonym, we mean simply something a customer can be persuaded to satisfy by spending money to buy what a salesperson offers.

For example, a woman looking at refrigerators in a store might murmur to her husband, or even to herself, "Oh, it's beautiful, but I really don't *need* a new refrigerator." What she means is that her present refrigerator is still working and doing its job, and she could manage for some time without a new one. Still, she is attracted to the idea of buying a new refrigerator, and if she decides she wants the refrigerator enough to part with the money or to obligate herself for the necessary payments, she has the "need" for that new refrigerator, as far as the salesperson is concerned. The question is: What will convert that passing interest in the new refrigerator into a need—into a decision to buy?

Getting that woman into the store, into the department, and admiring the new refrigerator is primarily the responsibility of marketing. Fanning that interest into desire and a sale is the responsibility of sales. Somewhere in this process the two functions are so closely related that it's hairsplitting to attempt to discriminate between them (which is probably why so many people confuse the two functions), but that is really not surprising when you consider that selling is part of—the final act in—marketing. In fact, the very success of selling activity is a mark of the effectiveness of the marketing effort, and a lack of sales success may well be a reflection of poor marketing, rather than poor selling.

Another way in which we might define marketing is this: Marketing is (in part, at least) identification of customer wants or needs. That is obviously a greatly simplified approach to understanding the marketing function, and there is a great deal more to a complete definition of the function, but marketing does begin with identifying needs. However, that term *need* has many levels of meaning, and no discussion of marketing can be very helpful without extensive exploration and understanding of the concept of customer needs.

First of all, we should recognize that every person has certain human needs which can be expressed in basic terms that make the need common to everyone. We all need food, clothing, shelter, love, security, heat, and so forth. For most of us, life without all of these is unthinkable.

How we satisfy those needs is another matter. The methods for satisfying needs vary according to a number of factors, at least these:

What is available.
What we can afford.
What we prefer as individuals.

Of course, a typewriter is an office necessity today because typewriters are available and no one would accept business correspondence that was not typed. For most offices today, an *electric* typewriter is a necessity; it would be difficult to sell anyone a manual typewriter for business use. We may not be far from the day when it will be difficult to sell anyone an electric typewriter for office use: It may be that everyone will find word processors indispensable.

Monopolies are rare. Xerox Corporation had a virtual monopoly because patent protection gave them a monopoly on plain-paper copiers for a number of years. But even then there were competitors who had at least some success in the marketplace. In the case of electric typewriters, IBM obviously leads the field. Yet there are IBM competitors who make satisfactory machines and enjoy some share of the market. This means that while more customers have a "need" for IBM typewriters than for other makes, there are many customers with a need for other makes of electric typewriter. But what are the differences of need that lead to sales of different makes of electric typewriter?

One difference of need is price, of course. Some customers have a need for a lower price, and will buy the electric typewriter that they believe has the lowest price attached to it. Price is a need, in many cases.

Another difference may be a technical difference. Perhaps one typewriter has some feature the others do not have, and the customer decides that the feature satisfies a need the other machines do not. That feature—perhaps automatic centering—is a need.

Another need might be speed of delivery. Perhaps one company is in a position to make immediate delivery, while another cannot promise delivery for several days or even weeks. For some customers, immediate delivery is a need.

The basic need, then, is for an electric typewriter, but how the need will be satisfied—which typewriter the customer will buy—will depend on other needs which are subsets of the basic need. In many cases, it is the identification of these other needs which determines ultimate success or failure in the marketplace, because they determine the success or failure of the sales effort.

As soon as it became available, xerographic copying proved so superior to thermographic, chemical, and other copying methods that it pushed all other methods out of the marketplace almost overnight. But among the many xerographic copying machines, only one could copy on plain paper because only one had the basic patent protection to the devices that made such copying possible. So while the competitive machines were xerographic, they all required the use of specially treated paper, a serious drawback. Far more customers felt a need for copying on plain paper than felt a need for lower costs or other features. In this case, there was nothing the competitors' marketing people could do because they simply could not satisfy the need for copying on plain paper until the patents expired. Ergo, their strategy was simply to do the best they could under the circumstances, and stay alive until those patents expired, after which they would be in a far better position to meet the most widely felt need in the copier market.

Quite often, a number of suppliers can meet the basic need equally well, and the market shares are divided according to how well the suppliers meet the secondary needs. In many product lines, there isn't five cents' worth of difference among the products of the leaders. Yet even in these cases, sometimes one company leads the pack by far—it enjoys the major share of the market. Why?

TANGIBLE VERSUS INTANGIBLE NEEDS

Remember that we defined *need* earlier as any factor that induces a customer to buy, whether the factor is need in the "must have" sense or in the "would like to have" sense. In fact, in many cases, the customer has a need that is so subtle the customer is not consciously aware of it! In a great many cases, for example, the customer has a real need to have great *confidence* in the seller—a need to *feel secure*.

There is at least one outstanding example of this in the well-known advertisements and TV commercials of a large insurance company which assures you that "you're in good hands" when you are insured by them. And they actually illustrate this idea by drawing a pair of hands cupped together so as to form a nest. Or is it more suggestive of a cradle?

In any case, the meaning is plain enough. The appeal is to the individual's need for a feeling of security, and it is quite blatant. But it apparently works; for if it didn't, we must assume, the company would have abandoned it in favor of some other message.

Institutional advertising—advertising that does not attempt to sell any specific term, but only to promote the image of the advertiser—is another example of this idea, although it is a far more subtle message. A large corporation will often run such advertisements, extolling its own virtues as a major pillar of strength in the economy and on the American scene in general. The objective of such promotion is simply to build the image of the advertiser so as to create public confidence in the company.

Another well-known commercial is that of another insurance company, which uses the Rock of Gibraltar as a symbol of its solidity and urges viewers to "get a piece of the Rock." Since being "as solid as Gibraltar" is a well-established cliché for dependability, the message comes across easily.

What is actually being sold here? In all cases, even those where the advertising is institutional and does not attempt to sell the advertiser's products or services directly, there is sales effort: The advertiser is selling an image—dependability, integrity, security, confidence. The listener/viewer/reader is assured that the advertiser is someone you can buy from with great confidence. For example, the advertiser may be a great corporation which has many divisions, some of them producing consumer products, other building space and weapons systems for the government. Frequently, such firms will advertise their accomplishments under huge government contracts, although they place such advertisements in consumer-oriented publications, where they will be read by individuals who have nothing to do with government contracts. The objective of such advertisements is to build consumer confidence in the great corporation so as to soften up the prospect for sales appeals by the corporation's consumer-products divisions. That is marketing—preparing the way for sales effort.

Of course, small businesses can't really afford this kind of marketing. It's expensive and affordable only by corporations who have excess profits and can establish huge advertising budgets. However, the philosophy of building customer confidence in the company—making the prospect *feel secure* in doing business with the company—is just as valid and useful here as in the case of the large corporation. The chief difference is simply that the smaller company must find ways to combine this type of marketing with direct advertising utilized to make sales. The need of a customer to feel secure in doing business with a seller is as real as the customer's need to realize the benefits of the purchase. However, the importance of the need varies with the importance of the purchase. Obviously, the customer spending a few dollars for a minor item— a necktie, for example—is not going to worry much about the integrity of the maker of the necktie. At the same time, a customer who is sufficiently style conscious might worry about the maker's reputation as a designer of smart and stylish items. Or about the retailer's dependability for standing behind their sales guarantees.

These, too, are concerns that fall into the general category of confidence and security. They are specific items about which customers are concerned, and which, intangible though they may be, are major factors in determining how much sales resistance a customer will exhibit. For it is specifically to break down sales resistance that businesses offer warranties and guarantees, and it is also to build customer confidence— to make them feel secure—that many retail stores spend great sums of money to create a "front" of expensive furnishings, deep carpeting, and other physical evidences of their commitment. The typical fur salon, for example, is expensively furnished; it usually has soft background music; glass and brass are carefully polished at least once a day; salespeople are tastefully dressed and speak in soft tones; and the entire atmosphere is a hushed one, suggestive of culture and money. That's because the items offered for sale are all quite expensive, and customer confidence is one of the most important factors in making sales.

On the other hand, there are establishments that strive for the opposite impression. A store claiming discounts and bargain prices attempts to create an atmosphere to support belief in these low prices. The Robert Hall clothing chain always spoke loudly of their "plain pipe rack" fixtures, to support belief in their claims of discount prices; and in today's discount supermarkets—a growing trend in recent years—most of the merchandise is simply stacked in cartons on the floor or, at best, displayed on the cheapest of racks and shelves. These stores do not even supply bags, although customers may use the empty cartons stacked near the checkout registers. These devices are used more to support the discount image than because the paper bags would actually add significantly to costs!

IMAGE AND CREDIBILITY

Another word for what we have been discussing here is *credibility*. Each business must have some basic underlying strategy. That entails a number of factors, of which image is one: The marketer must know what he wants the customer to perceive. All marketing must then be directed toward creating that image and making it a credible one. *Your* perception of your business is not worth two cents unless it agrees with the customer's perception. Or perhaps we ought to turn that around, and point out that you must somehow create a customer perception that fits the perception you have. The point is that only the customer's perception is important and has any direct bearing on how well your sales efforts do. If you are doing business under a canvas tent erected in a corner of a large parking lot, you will have some difficulty creating an image of solid dependability. Customers will not be willing to place much reliance on your guarantees without better evidence that you are likely to be around next month or next year. Therefore, even if you could get a manufacturer to supply you as a dealer, you'd have considerable difficulty selling furs or other big-tag items without an establishment that appeared to be founded well enough to be around for a while.

In the final analysis, most business failures are due, in part at least, to failures of marketing. Nothing destroys a business more rapidly and more surely than declining sales. The reverse is also true: Many businesses that are badly managed and guilty of numerous disastrous decisions survive simply because their basic marketing and sales activity is successful enough to enable them to surmount their other problems.

It's fairly common, for example, for multidivision corporations to have a number of divisions losing money, several which are marginal, and one or two which are so successful that they carry the rest of the corporation, including all the losers therein. (They also carry a load of bad managers, and shield them from the consequences of their own poor decision making.)

WHAT IS MARKETING?

Now that we have developed so many avenues, perhaps we are in a position to attempt a better definition of marketing than we were at the outset of these discussions. On the one hand, we want to distinguish between marketing and sales because it is necessary to make that distinction if we are to gain a good understanding of what marketing is and what it should do for the business. On the other hand, we don't want to lose sight of the fact that sales may properly be considered to be part of marketing—in fact, the objective of marketing—and best understood as the final act of the marketing process. Let us consider the major actions we must accomplish in carrying out an effective marketing function:

1. Determine what we are selling
2. Determine what the customer is buying (what business we're in).
3. Determine *who* we will sell to (who needs the results identified in item 2 above?).
4. Decide how we reach the "who" of item 3 to make our offers.
5. Decide *how* we persuade them to buy (image, sales arguments, etc.).
6. Plan the actual sales program.
7. Carry it out (implement the sales program).

Although we have touched on each of these topics briefly, we will explore each in greater depth in the chapters to come as we discuss what various entrepreneurs have done to implement their marketing and sales programs, and what other entrepreneurs can do. The basic philosophies apply to all businesses, but the methods vary widely according to the types of business and other circumstances.

One thing should be clearly understood: While there are many methods that may be applied, marketing is not a science. It is an art, which means that the methods must be adapted to individual circumstances, and your own imagination may turn out to be of greater value to you than anything this book can tell you. Never underestimate the power of your own creative imagination. It is probably your greatest asset—*provided you are not afraid to exercise it.*

3

Your Creative Imagination

*Marketing is both art and science and as art is
inevitably creative—or should be.*

IS CREATIVITY A NATURAL GIFT?

It is not by chance that children tend to be far more imaginative and
creative than adults. Everything in our Western society—educational
systems and other societal influences—discourage creative imagination
in us, and most of us tend to be less and less creative as we mature.
Moreover, it has been found that education discourages creativity to
such an extent that those with advanced degrees tend to shrink strongly
from innovative thoughts.

There are many reasons for this phenomenon, but in general our
values drive us toward conformity. In general, society rewards conformity and penalizes nonconformity. We hear such clichés as "To get along,
go along," "That's not the way we've always done it," and "Don't make
waves." All these expressions impart the same message: Don't attempt to
be different; don't think independently; don't fight the system. Do what
everyone else does; follow accepted standards; and don't draw attention
to yourself. Small wonder that in a society that preaches such ideas
almost universally, innovative thinkers are in an excruciatingly small
minority.

The human animal is indeed gifted with creativity and imagination; it's our conditioning that frightens these traits out of us. Yes,
frightens them out of us. It takes a great deal of courage to be different,
and being innovative or creative—to indulge in *any* independent
thinking—is being different, hence hazardous. All thinkers have had to
have courage. Alexander Graham Bell, Thomas Edison, Charles Ketter-
ing, Louis Pasteur, Robert Fulton, and countless other inventors and

creators were jeered at, denounced as fools—Ignaz Semmelweiss was persecuted in the midnineteenth century and actually was driven into a mental institution for having the temerity to advise medical practitioners that they must wash their hands between examinations of pregnant women if they were to avoid carrying infections from patient to patient. This was heresy in that day, but pregnant women were dying of puerperal fever in European hospitals, and doctors had not the faintest idea of why or how such deaths had become so common. They did not welcome being told that they were themselves the carriers of the disease.

Nor have we improved in more recent times. Join any established business organization and try to introduce new methods. You'll almost surely run into the "NIH" syndrome immediately. That means Not Invented Here, which in turn means that it must be unacceptable—or at the very least, highly suspect. It is not always the large organizations that resist new ideas; the smallest companies are as bad as the largest ones.

Military organizations are especially resistant to change, and many cavalry officers who could not give up their horses and take off their spurs before crawling into tanks and armored cars had to be retired. The classic case concerns the British Army, which attempted reorganization and modernization after the Second World War, with the intention of putting the lessons of that war to good use in improving British armed forces. In studying the various organizations of the army and their efficiency, it was discovered that no one knew the function of one private in each gun crew in artillery batteries. Since time immemorial, one soldier was detailed to stand to one side as the gun was fired, but no one could recall why the soldier was so detailed—what he was to do.

A great deal of research followed, including interviews with retired artillery officers and searches through the oldest field manuals that could be found. After a while, the answer was found: Originally, this soldier stood to one side to hold the horses' bridles and prevent their bolting when the gun was fired!

WHAT IS CREATIVITY?

In its essence, creation is a new combination; hence, creativity is the *ability* to make a new—and useful—combination. (If the new combination has no use, why bother to even discuss it?) The creative process refers to the means for making the new combination or to the steps taken in doing so.

Rarely is any creation or innovation totally and completely new. It is next to impossible to make something without using elements with which we are already familiar. When Charles Townes conceived the maser (which led to the laser), he was utilizing principles already known—for example, that particle motion slowed as temperature dropped and that this could be used to focus energy more efficiently. The Norton Company, a leader in the manufacture of grinding equipment, had its beginning over one hundred years ago when a young Swedish immigrant, Swen Pulson, became thoroughly disgusted with the messy glue and emery-powder grinding wheels used in those days to finish the pottery manufactured in the plant that employed him. He felt sure he could combine the emery powder with clay and fire it in a kiln to make a better grinding wheel. It took only three tries for him to succeed in making this new combination of known ideas work. And Clarence Birdseye didn't really "invent" frozen foods. Nature had already done that. Birdseye simply noted it, experimented a bit, and discovered what were the optimum temperatures at which to freeze various foods to best preserve their flavor. He then started Birdseye Seafoods, Inc., in New York City in 1923.

In each case the genius lay in foreseeing a need and opportunity, and assembling the correct experiences and know-how to create a means to satisfy the need and exploit the opportunity. In the cases cited here, creativity was put to work to create new products that were superior to anything else available then. However, as we proceed through these pages, we'll look also at many cases where creative talents were put to work to create better marketing ideas for a variety of established products and services. The principles of creativity work equally well in producing physical products, services, systems, literature, music, and almost anything else man aspires to. The roots of every creation lie in the past, in earlier experience. Most new inventions are improvements in older ones, but they could not have come about until after the older one had been created. The prior knowledge was an essential ingredient. Efforts were made to invent television nearly one hundred years ago; in fact, a crude model was built and television signals broadcast experimentally as long ago as 1910. However, electronics was simply not yet advanced enough, and—especially—there was not yet a suitable device for displaying the picture. It was only after the superheterodyne and the oscilloscope, with its cathode ray tube, had been invented, a number of years later, that modern television became possible. The oscilloscope was commercially successful in 1937, and practical television equipment was produced in 1941 (but the war suspended further progress until after 1945).

From this it should be evident that creativity is heavily dependent on knowledge of the past. To foresee what is possible in the future, one must know what has been possible in the past—and how it was accomplished, as well.

WHAT IT TAKES TO BE CREATIVE

It has already been stated that you must know what has already been done, and know it in detail, usually, if you are to be properly armed and equipped to create new and better ways. However, there are other requirements. One is the right mental attitude. You must always believe that there is a better way waiting to be found. You must believe that all things are possible. You must have great confidence in yourself and in your quest. You must have great courage, enough to ignore jeers and disparagement, enough to withstand disappointments and frustrations, enough to persevere, secure in the knowledge that you will eventually succeed.

Rarely does anyone succeed in anything on the first try. (If it was that easy, it would have been done by someone else long ago!) Almost without exception, accomplishing anything worthwhile—especially an innovative breakthrough of some sort—is undertaken against the odds, and requires time and repetitive effort. It is necessary to recognize that in advance and accept that you will have to pay that price to succeed.

Studies of the process of creativity reveal that three stages are involved in most innovative developments:

1. Concentration—intensive, conscious study of the problem and effort to devise a solution.
2. Incubation—consigning the problem to the subconscious mind and going on to other matters while the subconscious works on it.
3. Illumination—(also called inspiration) when the light suddenly goes on in your head and you have the answer, or at least the main key.

Of course, this does not mean that we do not often develop new ideas and come up with brilliant creations entirely through conscious effort. Many great new ideas are developed consciously and routinely. But a great many are the product of the subconscious mind rather than the conscious mind. Here is an example of how this process works: The other night, my wife got stuck trying to remember the name of an old friend she hadn't seen for a few years. She all but tore her hair out in frustration, trying to recall the name. Finally we went on to other matters. An hour later, she suddenly blurted out, "Howard West! That's it!"

All that had happened—and probably similar things have happened to you—is that when she was trying hard to remember the name, that was concentration. When she abandoned the effort and went on to other things, that was incubation: She had assigned the job of remembering the name to her subconscious mind. And when the subconscious interrupted her conscious thoughts to give her the answer, that was illumination.

If you have ever awakened in the middle of the night with a bright idea, that is another manifestation of illumination. Or if you have ever awakened in the morning with a bright new idea or the answer to a vexing problem, that is still another case of inspiration—a message from your subconscious mind.

Somehow, our subconscious is often far better at creating than our conscious mind. Perhaps that is because the subconscious is not afraid of jeers and ridicule, but probably at least part of the reason is that the subconscious mind has far better recall than does the conscious mind. (That's why most people can recall things under hypnosis that they cannot recall deliberately or in their normal, conscious state.) Of course, better recall means a better ability to review stored knowledge and seek out promising new combinations, which is what we are trying to do. Ergo, a great many inventive people, interviewed to study creativity, offer evidence that they get a great deal of assistance from their subconscious minds. There seems to be no doubt of this.

Among twenty-eight inventors who responded to a questionnaire sent out by Joseph Rossman, a U.S. patent examiner studying the psychology of the inventor, six said that they developed their ideas unconsciously, twelve stated that their ideas came to them while they were resting or relaxing, and ten said that they habitually got their ideas "out of the blue." Another researcher, Rudolf Flesch, reported on a number of cases in which inspiration came when the individual was not concentrating on the problem; in many cases, inspiration came when the individual was relaxing. Still another research team, R. Baker and W. Platt, report that 41 percent of the respondents to their questionnaire stated that they got their scientific hunches from subconscious or unconscious thought.

There is much other evidence along the same lines, enough to make the case beyond reasonable doubt. But there are other factors, too, and it is worthwhile to have a look at them. These include emotional factors—although others are involved, principally as motivators. Rossman's study included sending a questionnaire to each of 710 inventors. Among the responses to questions designed to probe the respondents' motivations, Rossman found the following:

193 expressed a simple love of inventing new devices.
189 wanted to improve existing devices.
167 were not motivated for financial gain.
118 said they had a practical need.
73 expressed a simple desire to achieve.
59 said it was just part of their job.
27 were interested in prestige.
22 professed altruistic reasons.

Without a doubt, a factor for success is confidence in a successful outcome. Researches have verified that innovators who succeed are almost invariably only those who believe in what they are doing and believe in ultimate success. Those who lack such faith simply do not persevere long enough to succeed. However, another factor found to be an essential is *visualization*.

VISUALIZATION

Someone has said, "What the mind can conceive, man can achieve." That's just another way of saying that you have to be able to visualize your goal—see it in your mind—and you will be able to reach it. That act of visualization helps you greatly to develop the confidence you need. It's as though you can't really believe it until you have painted a mental image.

Of course, you must have established a goal first. (How can you get anywhere if you don't know where you are trying to get?) You must visualize that goal in graphic detail, as well as all the major steps you know you will have to traverse to reach that goal. Write out the goal description in detail, as one means of visualizing. Don't set your sights too low; you can't hit a star by aiming at the moon. Set *worthy* targets for yourself; you're far more capable than you think!

HOW "NEW" DOES AN IDEA HAVE TO BE?

John D. Rockefeller, one of America's most successful business tycoons, often advised others against innovation. He believed that the most reliable and sensible way to business success was to observe what someone else was doing successfully and then emulate that success. Whether Mr. Rockefeller meant that advice to be taken literally or not is uncertain. However, logic suggests that he meant to counsel others to be guided by what is already working successfully and to avoid the highly chancy business of investing effort and money in completely new and untried ideas. Certainly it is not likely that he was counseling anyone to try to ape a successful enterprise in each and every particular, to create a Chinese copy of that success. In fact, this rarely works, for a number of reasons:

1. The two sets of conditions are not exactly the same.
2. Your own personality, preferences, and talents are unique, not the same as anyone else's.
3. You can't beat someone else at his or her own game.

In short, yes, do be guided by what you can learn from watching a successful enterprise, but don't let that keep you from exercising a bit of imagination, to adapt that enterprise to your own situation and circumstances. You have a far better chance of succeeding if and when you inject a bit of yourself into the enterprise. Don't sell your own capabilities short.

EVOLUTION, NOT REVOLUTION

The Wright brothers' heavier-than-air flying machine was a revolutionary development. Dramatically enough, and despite all criticism and the fact that they were not trained scientists or engineers, there was suddenly a proven accomplishment.

Less dramatic and sudden, although not in public perception, were such developments as the computer and the television receiver. The public could not know the painful, step-by-step evolutionary process through which these products were developed. As far as the public was concerned, they appeared suddenly and dramatically where nothing of the sort had existed before. Of course, because such events are dramatic, they make colorful copy for writers. This misleads the public into believing that all such developments are revolutionary—springing into existence suddenly. Perhaps this misleads you into believing that creativity and innovation must be revolutionary, producing sudden and dramatic change. Not so. Most change comes about gradually with new products, new systems, and new ideas coming into being slowly.

Fortunately, as far as changes that make for business success are concerned, slight and gradual improvements are usually sufficient. Many a business fortune has been founded on a relatively small change in some process, product, or idea. Ray Kroc, for example, did not invent the hamburger joint. Hamburger emporiums, such as the White Tower chain, had long existed and operated successfully, if not spectacularly. When Ray Kroc bought the right to the McDonald name and launched the McDonald hamburger chain, he made relatively slight improvements: He franchised first in Chicago, but put the franchise on a national basis; he set up firm controls so that all McDonald restaurants not only looked alike, but served the same food, prepared the same way; and he made sure that the restaurants were spotlessly clean throughout, with adequate rest room facilities. Most important of all, he launched a brilliant advertising and publicity campaign, which created a new industry, soon known as "fast foods."

Take the case of Steve Savage, of Vermont, as a more modest (but highly successful) example. Steve is in the business of supplying merchandise and related support to fund raisers, particularly to schools that raise funds by having students sell merchandise to individuals in the community. One of the several things Steve did to gain success was to change a practice other suppliers pursued: They would not take back unsold merchandise, forcing the fund raisers to "eat" anything they failed to sell. Steve agreed to take back anything unsold. He also sought and found a line of merchandise that sold well, but was not bulky or heavy. These changes and others that *helped his customers succeed* contributed to his own success.

Charles N. Aronson manufactured welding positioners in Arcade, New York—machines that sold for rather large sums of money in their larger sizes. (Some of the positioners were huge.) Two reasons for Aronson's success in selling machines that were more expensive than his competitors' was that he 1) offered much faster delivery than did most of his competitors and 2) always delivered on schedule, which his competitors rarely did.

Rockefeller's advice is good advice, then, if you both adopt (a successful idea) and adapt (modify it to your own needs). But the adaptation should not be for the purpose of suiting your own convenience; rather, it must be for the purpose of improving the idea and making it work in your situation. That is, when you study what others are doing successfully, study also what you (and, presumably, the customers) do not like about how that business is conducted. Decide what can and should be changed to improve it. Even a small change may make the difference between failure and success, or between modest success and sensational success.

Ivory soap is a good example of what a small change can mean. The difference between Ivory and other white soaps is, principally, that Ivory is full of air bubbles. That's what makes it float, and is also what got it so much attention and made it such an outstanding success for so many years. Moreover, the air bubbles were the result of a mistake—a workman who forgot to turn off the stirring machine when he went to lunch so that the soap mixture was agitated far longer than it should have been. But when people began asking for "that soap that floats," the soapmaker knew he was onto something big. Serendipity, to be sure, but the soapmaker was an entrepreneur who was smart enough to take advantage of the accident.

When hair sprays were introduced, they were rather costly. As they proved to be a popular item, many cosmetic manufacturers introduced their own brands. One introduced a spray at eighty-nine cents, a bargain price. It didn't sell, to the mystification of the manufacturer, who was sure that it equaled the others in quality and other characteristics. He called in a marketing consultant, who studied the situation briefly and then recommended one small change: The price was too low, and customers mistrusted the product. (When the customer has nothing else by which to judge quality, he is likely to judge by the price, as compared with the price of the competition!) When the price was raised to the same level as that of the competing hair sprays, sales began to climb.

The simple change that turned Montgomery Ward from just another retailer into the billion-dollar enterprise it became was this: Montgomery Ward pioneered the satisfaction-guaranteed-or-your-money-back offer in a day when such a thing was unheard of. His competitors were quite sure he was mad. But customers reacted positively and did not disappoint Ward: They did not take undue advantage of his generous guarantee, and Ward's success was so great that ultimately the guarantee became *de rigueur* in retailing; you could not do business without such a guarantee.

Note the significant factor about these changes that resulted in such spectacular business successes: In each case, the change was made with a view to accommodating the customer's interest. Ray Kroc was sure that travelers on the highways would appreciate having clean rest room facilities that they could absolutely depend on if they stopped at a McDonald's. Steve Savage eliminated much of the risk in fund-raising sales for his customers. Charles Aronson gave far better service to his customers and enabled them to plan absolutely for the day when the new machine would be delivered. Ivory soap pleased the customer, who liked the idea that the soap floated. Montgomery Ward took the risk out of buying by mail for his customers. And even the hair-spray maker served his customer's interests when he raised the retail price, because he set the customer's mind at rest about the quality of the product, something no amount of rationale could have done. That tells you something about the changes to be made—those changes that are most likely to be beneficial to you, as an entrepreneur: Make those changes most likely to provide some benefit to your customers. Here are some of the kinds of changes to consider when you are studying a business idea:

> Improvement in a product or service.
> Improvement in packaging of a product or service.
> Faster delivery.
> Greater convenience in ordering.
> Better guarantee.
> Better image, heightened customer confidence.
> Reduced price.

It is not by chance that reduced price is listed last. Reducing prices is the weakest of appeals. It suggests that you can think of no other compelling reason for prospects to become your customers. True, there are some customers to whom nothing is so appealing as the lowest price, but they are very much in the minority. At least high prices, if they are not out of reason, have never been the direct cause for business failure, as long as the business succeeded in demonstrating goods and/or services that were worth the price. There are always enough customers around who are willing to pay a fair price for whatever appeals sufficiently to them. It is not only the wealthy who patronize the "tonier" department stores, for example; the patronage of Bloomingdale's and Lord & Taylor includes an ample number of blue-collar workers and other middle-class citizens.

Those who advocate emulating existing success and those who advocate being original are both correct. Use demonstrated success as a basis for developing business ideas, but put your creative imagination to work to improve on what you observe and make it work better. That does not mean drastic change, either—the change may be quite small, yet produce large results.

The way to discover or invent changes that are improvements is to search for problems—for whatever is not working well. When you solve a common problem, you have discovered a way to satisfy a need. And when you can satisfy a need, you have the basis for a successful business enterprise, for that is what business is all about: solving people's problems and satisfying their needs.

Being creative means unchaining your mind. Most of us have our minds chained to something called conventional wisdom—what "everybody knows" and how "it's always been done." That is deadly conservatism, and it is not even logical. The reason so many people cling to that kind of thinking is because it involves a minimum of personal risk: You are not likely to be criticized if you stick with the established ways. Neither are you likely to accomplish a great deal. Think about it. If we never considered new ideas, would we not still be living in caves and eating raw meat? Developing new ideas and *putting them to work* is known as *progress*. Find a business—any business—that is doing exactly what it was doing five or more years ago, and you have found a business on the decline. It has long been recognized that death and taxes are inevitable. To that you may add change: Change is inevitable. Those who do not change, perish—especially in business. It's been happening frequently and to companies that were considered large, solid, and well established. They failed to change, and they were ridden down by competitors who were changing, who overtook them and trampled them in the dust.

Change requires courage. It is the timid and fearful who cling to the old ways stubbornly, irrationally—and fatefully. But change is self-preservation, for reasons just explained: If you fail to change as needed, your business days are surely numbered.

Change requires awareness. You must keep up, know your industry, know what's happening in the marketplace. That means, in the final analysis, you must know what people are thinking, what customers are buying. *Customers* are "the market." If there is a market for jeans, that simply means that a great many customers wish to buy jeans. Again and again, the garment industry deceives themselves into believing they can dictate fashion, and the results are such fiascos as the Nehru jacket, maxicoat, and midiskirt. Sellers don't create markets; customers create markets, and sellers—smart sellers—react appropriately. You must keep a finger on the pulse of the market to know what changes are likely to be beneficial.

Marketing is not an exact science. (It's not even an inexact science, to be truthful!) It's far more art than science, and this means that the gifted marketer relies on instinct, judgment, and other subtle factors that are difficult to rationalize except as hunches or instincts. To have those brilliantly successful hunches and instincts, it is necessary to know your business—and your business is marketing. But just what does that mean? It certainly means more than knowing the principles of salesmanship, although there appears to be a great number of people who call themselves marketers and whose special knowledge is, in fact, confined primarily to a knowledge of sales techniques and tactics. No, knowing your business as a marketer means knowing your business along several lines of knowledge, which include technical knowledge of your industry as well as knowledge of sales, advertising, psychology, and a few other subjects. That is, if you are marketing ice cream, you ought to know something about how ice cream is made, how it is distributed, the differences among various brands and grades, costs, and many other things about ice cream as a product and as an industry. On the other hand, if you are marketing for a department store or general-merchandise chain, it is not likely that you are going to be an expert in all lines of merchandise, but you certainly ought to know the department-store industry (if I may refer to it as an industry). You must know, for example, what kinds of goods are moving best, which are slumping (that is, which goods the customers are showing interest in and which they are not), and other matters of critical importance.

Irvine Robbins, of Baskin-Robbins ice cream fame, discovered early in his career that when he sold ice cream through supermarkets, each store sold only a modest volume of his ice cream—as one of many food items, they didn't push it very enthusiastically. But when he sold ice cream through ice cream stores, who had nothing else to sell—boy, could they sell ice cream! And because Robbins markets just one thing, Baskin-Robbins ice cream, he is an expert on ice cream and the industry.

On the other hand, Stanley Marcus, whose father co-founded the famous Neiman-Marcus store in Dallas, ultimately became an expert in many items—for example, furs—but he had to rely on his various buyers for product expertise, for the most part, while he furnished the department-store-retailing expertise. The younger Marcus, by the way, developed and contributed a great many innovative small changes that added to the store's success, although the two founders had done quite well in that field also.

Frank Perdue, of the Perdue chickens, has become a well-known personality as a result of doing his own commercials on TV and on the radio. This was not because he wanted to economize in his advertising costs, but because the commercials proved to be most effective when he did them himself with his distinctive and nonprofessional-sounding voice. (When a professional announcer or narrator did the commercials, they were simply unconvincing.) If there is a single distinguishing feature of the Perdue campaign, it is the concentration on the pronounced, desirable yellow color of Perdue chickens, as compared with the white color of most other chickens.

Tom Carvel—of Carvel ice cream—is another entrepreneur who finds that his commercials work best when he does them himself, in his own scratchy, somewhat unpleasant voice, inflicting mayhem on grammar and pronunciation as well as on diction. But Carvel says he has no actor's ego because he's working steadily, and that's what's most important to him. He is quick to assure his interviewer that his real name is not Carvel, but Carvelas, and he hastens to explain that Carvelas is Greek. He looks a good bit like an aging Adolph Menjou, especially when he grins, as he explains a few facts about his business. It becomes abundantly clear that he, too, is an expert par excellence on ice cream.

AN IMPORTANT FINAL POINT

There is one most important point to make before we go on to discuss various types of business enterprise, and that is a reiteration: Although we have discussed creativity, innovation, and constructive change in general, we have not left our main subject, which is marketing. It's all marketing. Anything that helps capture a customer's attention, breaks down sales resistance, breaks trail for a salesperson, or gives a customer the slightest additional reason to notice you and become interested in what you offer is marketing. It is important that you never lose sight of that. Customers are what a business is all about, for without them there is no business.

4

Marketing
for Different Types
of Enterprises

*Just as there are many kinds of enterprises, there
are many ways to market. There is a need to
match the two for best results.*

A FIRST STEP IN DECIDING
WHAT BUSINESS YOU'RE IN

There are a great many kinds of enterprises among the nearly fourteen
million businesses in the United States. However, despite the number of
different enterprises, most if not all are based on one of the following
three basic propositions:

> Creation of goods.
> Sale of goods created by someone else.
> Provision of services.

Let's have a look at different types of enterprise—and we'll look at a
fairly large number, although not all, by any means—and see if we can
fit them fairly into one of those three most basic classes just listed.

Manufacturing—Pretty obviously the creation of goods.

Mining—Also creation of goods. (See why I didn't use *manufacturing* as the basic category?) Mining, by the way, includes the extraction of
any mineral from the earth, including petroleum.

Farming—Farmers obviously create goods to be sold, as do ranchers
and commercial fishers and hatchers, which I include here as being
virtually the same as farmers.

Food Processing—Baking, making ice cream and candy, and similar
enterprises are manufacturing, as far as I am concerned, and belong in
this same category of creation of goods.

Restaurants—It seems to me that restaurants also process food, starting usually with raw material, to create finished meals, despite the fact that they also buy much of the food already finished. I classify this enterprise as the creation of goods, although a case can be made for it as a service enterprise too.

Publishing—Creation of goods because it processes the author's raw material into a finished product to be sold. (Later, we will talk about a kind of publishing that could be considered to be strictly a service.)

Retailing—Clearly, selling goods others create.

Wholesaling—Also selling goods created elsewhere, and this includes such enterprises as jobbing and distributing, which are the same thing as wholesaling.

Franchising—I consider this to be a service, although franchising may include selling certain items to franchisees. Essentially, however, a franchiser is selling the pulling power of an established name, a business system, training and guidance, and technical support, all of which are services.

Dry Cleaning—Clearly a service.

Computer Programming—A service primarily, although a product is involved (the physical document that represents the program, which is in the form of a magnetic tape most commonly today). The customer is buying the product, of course, but virtually the entire cost charged to the customer is to pay for the service required to develop that product. The same may be said for analogous custom work—preparing engineering drawings, designing a product, custom writing, illustrating, etc.

Publishing—Some kinds of publishing are really much more the provision of a service than the creation of goods. Publishing books (or any other publication) for mass distribution is a manufacturing operation, with the development costs distributed across a large number of sales—amortized rather than billed to a single customer for whom the cost was incurred. However, the production of a newsletter for a limited number of customers or the development of a special report for a limited number of customers is somewhat different philosophically. Instead of selling the publication per se, you are really selling *information,* and many would consider that a service.

Consulting—Most consulting is selling information, most definitely, even when the consultant provides other services than information; definitely a service enterprise.

Undertaking—Undertakers—or morticians, as some prefer to be called—offer a service, in my opinion, despite the high prices most charge for the physical devices provided. However, those are really incidental to the main functions the mortician is expected to perform; ergo, my conviction that this enterprise is definitely a service.

There are many enterprises on the borderline, as are some of the above. Is it important that we sort and classify each enterprise in this manner? Yes, to the extent it is important that you, as the entrepreneur, have a clear understanding of what business you are in—what, exactly, the customer is buying from you. Here are a few more. Make your own best estimate as to how you would classify each of these:

Moviemaking: _____

Selling Recipes: _____

Drawing a Syndicated Cartoon Strip: _____

Operating a Vending Machine Route: _____

Repackaging a Bulk Product in Small Packages for Resale: _____

Don't read on until you have decided all of the above. Then you may read on and find out what I think the right answers are.

MY ANSWERS

I think that moviemaking can be classified as either the creation of goods or the selling of service. If you make a commercial kind of movie—one that you finance and sell or rent by the copy, in the hope that you will sell or rent enough to recover all costs and turn a profit (or maybe even make a lot of money, if you get lucky)—that's certainly creating goods for sale. It's a speculation entailing risk and with the possibility of making a *lot* of money. On the other hand, if you make a movie of the type usually called an industrial movie, for another party, billing the customer all your costs plus your profit and passing all ownership and rights to the customer, you are being paid to provide a service; the goods are strictly incidental.

Selling recipes is definitely a service business: It's selling information, of course.

Drawing a syndicated cartoon strip or writing a syndicated column is something like the moviemaking problem: It can be fairly regarded as either a service enterprise or the creation of sale of goods. However, considering the way syndicated material is sold (as many copies, at moderate per-copy prices), it seems fair to regard this enterprise as the creation of goods, with the customer buying the product rather than the service.

Operating a route of vending machines is nothing more than selling merchandise at retail. It's selling goods created by others.

There are entrepreneurs who buy things in bulk—tea, for instance —and package it for resale either at wholesale or retail. In fact, such entrepreneurs are creating goods, even if they are not doing anything more than measuring and packaging a product created by someone else. The customer will regard the package of tea as your product.

WHAT DIFFERENCE DOES IT MAKE?

Deciding which of the above categories your enterprise properly belongs in is a first step in understanding what business you are in or are considering. If you are going to market successfully, you must first have an accurate vision of what you are really selling—that is, what the customer is willing to pay for. Let's consider those different kinds of enterprise from that viewpoint.

CREATION OF GOODS

Creating goods—being known as a prime source, in some business circles—includes manufacturing, agriculture, food processing, and just about any enterprise in which you purchase materials in one form and sell them in some other form; that would include hobby and handicraft activities, too. There are gray areas in which it is not a clear-cut decision. The difficulty arises principally when you try to make this analysis and judgment from your viewpoint as an entrepreneur. The view is somewhat different when you make the analysis from the customer's viewpoint, and *that is the viewpoint you must adopt.*

The significant point in identifying what business you are in is putting your finger on exactly what the customer is buying, regardless of what you are selling—or think you are selling. *It's only by knowing exactly what the customer is buying that you can market effectively and build your business.*

Let's take that restaurant business as an outstanding example of how difficult it is to make a blanket decision that all enterprises of some specified category are one thing or the other. As examples of two extremes, consider a typical fast-food establishment versus an elegant dining room in an exclusive hotel. Do you have any difficulty believing that patrons of these two establishments have selected the establishment they want to eat in for entirely different reasons—that is, that each of the two establishments is selling something entirely different from the other? The fast-food establishment is principally selling price, and to a lesser extent, speedy service. Perhaps some of the patrons are there because they want to gulp a quick lunch, but if you study typical patrons in such an establishment, you won't find very much evidence that the patrons are all in a great rush to eat and get going. It's almost certain that the chief appeal of fast-food restaurants is to the pocketbook. Only in competing with each other do fast-food chains attempt to gain patronage on the basis of claimed superiority of food and service; when the appeal is clearly in competition with more formal dinner restaurants, it is directed to the pocket, the lower-price appeal.

On the other hand, that exclusive hotel and its white-tablecloth-and-shining-crystal characteristics can hardly appeal to the pocketbook or to a desire for fast service. It must find other motivators to attract patrons—and while as a class these may be entirely different patrons from those pursued by the marketers of fast foods, individual diners in the hotel dining room may very well have had their lunch in a McDonald's or Gino's! In the restaurant business, dinner and lunch are frequently two entirely different markets, although the customers for each may be the same individuals.

In any case, the formal dinner restaurant, if it is a name place or one that might be called tony or high-toned, depends primarily on something that is frequently called ambience or atmosphere. The appeal is to the kind of person who wants to dine in a relaxed but somewhat formal environment, usually with a predinner cocktail, maximum service from well-trained servers, and immaculate cloths, silver, dishes, and glassware. In many cases, management has gone to great expense to create some special, distinctive atmosphere, which may be ethnic, foreign, regional, or just continental. In some cases, the restaurant may specialize in a certain kind of food—seafoods, Mexican food, Italian food, Middle Eastern food, and so on. Or it may be a general or continental restaurant that has different "nights," each devoted to offering specialized, regional, or ethnic dishes.

In some cases, a restaurant becomes an in place where patrons go to see and be seen. In New York, for example, there were once a great many such restaurants. A notice in a popular column, such as that of Walter Winchell or Ed Sullivan, would mean instant success for the restaurant, for patrons would begin to swarm there, expecting to see and be seen.

Some restaurants would be harmed by such a notice because their patronage was by wealthy people who did not want to be gawked at by tourists, as they feared they would be if the restaurant became too popular by being publicized in newspaper columns. Such restaurants had a snob appeal, and their patronage grew through intelligence on the grapevine that they were "in" places of a special kind.

Perhaps the past tense is not properly used here because such establishments are not all gone, although there are not nearly as many as there once were, and most of those that were once well known are no more in New York City. The point, however, is still entirely valid: Patrons go to different kinds of restaurants for different kinds of reasons, and the marketer who wants to market a restaurant effectively must make an accurate appraisal of how the given establishment can appeal most effectively.

We have used extremes here: the typical fast-food, "one arm" joint versus the high-toned, usually exclusive and expensive dining room. Extreme examples were used to dramatize the main point and make it crystal clear. However, there are literally millions of small restaurants in the United States that fall between these two extremes. These are the really difficult enterprises to classify, as a prelude to effective marketing. However, let's first take a quick look at the characteristics of these two extremes, as their marketers attempt to satisfy their patrons' wants.

All restaurant patrons want to be assured that they are eating in sanitary surroundings, that the food is handled with proper regard for sanitation and general cleanliness, that the food is of high quality, and so forth. So all restaurants, regardless of what kind of patronage they are trying to attract, must work at creating such impressions. In the typical fast-food restaurant, the entire place is designed, usually, to convey an impression of and actually achieve a high degree of efficiency. Moreover, it is generally arranged so that it can be kept clean easily, using tile floors, stainless steel counters, paper and plastic utensils and serving plates, and handily located trash barrels. Of course, such places are geared to self-service with a wide counter, behind which is the kitchen, almost totally exposed to view.

That tony dining room provides superior table service; the kitchen cannot be seen by the patrons; the floors are carpeted; the tables are covered with spotless, crisp linen; and so on. The general effect sought is that of luxury. Heavy drapes and carpeting muffle echoes so that the atmosphere is hushed, with a comfortable background of murmuring voices, laughter, and the tinkle of silver and glassware. In some cases there may be dinner music playing softly in the background.

If patrons go to the fast-food place to eat swiftly and inexpensively, they come to this dining room to enjoy the company, the atmosphere, and the food, as much as to satisfy hunger. The food may or may not be superior in quality of preparation, but it probably tastes good because the entire atmosphere encourages the belief that the food is A-1 in all respects: A patron almost *dare not* think that such an establishment would serve anything but the best! Creating that impression, through creating a proper ambience, is marketing. It shows an understanding of why the patron is there and what the patron wishes to buy.

The fast-food place is a mass producer—manufacturer—of hamburgers and fried chicken . . . by the plate or by the bucket . . . eat it here or take it home. It's fast and it's cheap, and the enterprise depends on volume: Get 'em in and get 'em out, as quickly as possible. "Fast" is not entirely for the patrons' benefit, although we'll never tell them that; it's also for our own benefit: We can't make any money if we don't keep them moving. It takes a certain minimum volume of hamburgers, french fries, fried chicken, milk shakes, and Cokes to pay the rent and the help and leave something over for the owner.

In the final analysis the customer is buying a service, of course, as all customers are, no matter what, where, and under what circumstances they buy anything. The customer is buying a full and contented stomach and hoping that the experience of getting a full and contented stomach will be reasonably pleasurable, although one is not naive enough to expect a gastronomic *tour de force*. For the most part, the customer is buying an *inexpensively* achieved full and contented stomach and, perhaps, a minimum sacrifice of time from a busy schedule. (After all, lunch time is taken from the busy business day, whereas dinner is ordinarily after the end of the business day, when one can take time and relax.) So, viewed in that manner, it seems not unreasonable to see the fast-food restaurant operation as the creation of goods which customers wish to buy. Many do, in fact, prefer the drive-up-and-eat-in-your-car convenience, which is even more clearly indicative of an enterprise that creates goods to be purchased as goods by the customer.

It seems fairly clear, then, that certain kinds of restaurants sell products they create, while other kinds sell a service as their primary appeal. It is difficult to draw a sharp dividing line between the two types of eating establishment, except as we approach the extremes. So many restaurants fall somewhere along a rather broad spectrum of types of eating establishments in the middle; these include cafeterias and other fast-food places that are not elements of restaurant chains or franchisees, many of which have counter service only, which may be classed as diners or call themselves family restaurants, serving full dinners but sans white linen and deep carpets, and (of course) at far more modest prices than are listed on the oversize menu cards placed in front of diners at "Maison Elegante." There are even tiny hamburger stands and their gastronomic relatives, which also qualify technically as restaurants.

So it is not easy to segregate restaurants into those that specialize in manufacturing food items whose business is the volume sale of those food items, and those whose business is selling the service of dinner-hour grace and pleasure. Except at or near the extremes discussed here, there are huge numbers of restaurants that represent a compromise between these extremes, appealing to those who can't or refuse to afford the costly white-linen-and-polished-silver dining room but want something a bit more gracious than a mass-produced hamburger or chicken breast served on a throwaway plate. Patrons of these in-between-the-extremes kinds of eating establishments are presumably customers seeking to be served, with some degree of comfort and grace, but at considerably lower prices than would be exacted in fancier restaurants.

So if we are to segregate the restaurant patrons into three distinct groups, we have these descriptions and marketing approaches:

Those who buy mass-produced food either because of low price or fast service (possibly both), and whose patronage is gained, presumably, by appealing to such desires and promising to satisfy them.

Those who want eating to be a pleasant experience in comfortable surroundings, possibly because they have an ego need to be seen in the most exclusive or most expensive dining rooms in town, and are not deterred by the cost of such luxury. Such patrons are attracted by appeals to the ego, by stressing the exclusivity of the establishment, by making it clear that the establishment offers the finest of continental-quality service and exquisitely prepared foods, and by stressing the relaxed and gracious atmosphere—the ambience that patrons of such places expect.

For that third group that falls between these extremes, the basic marketing appeal should be toward those patrons who want to relax and enjoy their dinners, who buy the *service* of a table-service dinner restaurant, but with certain variations: For one thing, the appeal must make clear that prices are not excessively high, but are within the presumed means of the average middle-class family; for another, snob appeal does not work here—the patron wants to relax and enjoy a meal that is well prepared and properly served. Those features should be stressed. If the establishment specializes in some ethnic or regional dishes—Italian, Mexican, Chinese, etc.—that should also be made clear. Usually such establishments stress that the food is authentically valid as representative of that country or ethnic group. But to avoid screening out some patrons, many such establishments also stress that "American dishes" are available. Precisely how such messages are transmitted in the marketing activities will become evident as we progress.

It must not be supposed that only the restaurant business poses this problem of different target populations of customers and customer prospects. Many businesses are or can be so varied in their specializations as to pose the same problems of how to identify the most viable customer potential and how to persuade these people to become customers. Publishing is one such industry, as has been briefly mentioned earlier. There are publishers of books, publishers of periodicals, publishers of newsletters, and publishers of special products, such as reports. Even then, each class subdivides. Book publishers may publish almost any type of book or they may specialize. Periodical publishers may publish a single publication or they may publish several, and they may publish on a somewhat leisurely quarterly basis or on the frenetic daily basis of a newspaper. Newsletter publishers similarly may publish on a leisurely quarterly basis or on a frantic daily basis. (It may occur to you to wonder why newsletter publishing is not included under periodical publishing; it's because newsletter publishing is so different in so many ways from publishing a newspaper or magazine.) And publishers of special products have the freedom to publish almost anything that strikes them as having a profit potential.

In these days of swift and inexpensive offset printing, plus the acceptability of type set by electric typewriter, publishing has become possible for the smallest entrepreneur, and there are many individuals operating publishing enterprises from their homes, even on a spare-time basis. For the most part, these entrepreneurs publish newsletters and small reports, which they sell by mail. In a few cases, such publishers also publish small books, usually paperbound books of 50 to 150 pages, sometimes typeset but often typewriter set.

The book publisher who produces a relatively large number of books per year—perhaps twenty-five to fifty new titles, but in some cases several hundred new titles annually—may also distribute books by mail, but often sells trade editions. (This means, simply, that the books are sold through bookstores—through the trade.) And publishers of textbooks generally use traveling salespeople, referred to frequently as travelers.

Publishers of periodicals, principally magazines—which may be weekly or monthly, although a few are biweekly, bimonthly, or quarterly —may distribute their products by mail, on newsstands, or via both methods. This depends primarily on whether the publication is a "popular" one—appealing to a large number of people—or highly specialized, appealing only to a relatively select few.

Newspaper publishers are a special case, as are newsletter publishers. Most often daily or weekly, newspapers get the bulk of their distribution via home delivery and newsstands, although some have large numbers of subscribers to whom they mail copies.

If we are to classify publishing in terms of these three general classifications we set up earlier, we would find that publishing has a number of different classes of customers (in terms of what they want to buy or why they buy the items they do), much as the restaurant business has. Here are the broad, basic kinds of customers, in terms of what they seek:

There is the customer seeking simple diversion or escape. This customer buys fiction, general-interest magazines, general-interest nonfiction. Of course, this kind of customer can be subdivided according to tastes (e.g., readers of romances, lovers of mysteries, and so on) and also according to whether they customarily buy cloth-bound (hard-cover) editions or paperback editions.

There is also the customer seeking information in some special category. This can include students, of course, but can be almost anyone having either a vocational or avocational interest in some subject.

There is the browser, who pokes around in a book store or at a newsstand with no special purpose, but ready to have his or her interest piqued by anything on the shelf, and ready to buy anything of interest.

Many of these customers are strictly buyers of a created product—they buy books, magazines, and newspapers, motivated by interest and often by price. That is, this class of customer may or may not buy a given book, according to its price, but will seek out a book or magazine that arouses interest but is within some given price range.

There are those customers who are seekers after information of a special sort, and who will pay a relatively high price for a book or magazine, but will examine the book or magazine carefully to make comparisons among several books (e.g., dictionaries), seeking the best buy.

There are customers who are strictly buying information—a service—and will pay whatever is required to get the service. These are the buyers of costly newsletters, which are produced on typewriters and by inexpensive offset printing on inexpensive paper. It is the information they seek, not the product per se, and they are well aware that they are paying for a service. (Frequently, highly specialized newsletters have only a few hundred subscribers, making the subscription price unavoidably high, but still acceptable to those who want the information badly enough.)

Here again, the appeals are different for each of these classes of customers. Some are reached by stress on the content of a book or magazine, promising exciting drama, breathtaking conflict, and so on. Some news magazines stress the style of the writing staff, as well as the in-depth coverage and timeliness of the news stories. Rarely is price stressed, although it is carefully considered in marketing the product. Brand name—the publisher's identity, that is—is rarely a motivating factor with book buyers, but author's name is frequently a key factor: Many readers will almost automatically buy anything new written by a favorite author.

Another factor is how customers buy. There are those who prefer to subscribe to their favorite periodicals or who will buy books by mail or through book clubs. But there are also those who will buy periodicals only from a newsstand, or who will buy books only after browsing through a book store. Marketing must recognize, in devising suitable appeals, that customers are classed in this manner also. In fact, many people enjoy browsing as part of the book-buying process, and will not forego this pleasure by ordering through the mail.

So while publishing is essentially the selling of a created product, some customers of published products are buying a service rather than a product, and can be persuaded to buy by stressing the service provided rather than the product itself.

On the other hand, selling specific products created for specific—and usually quite obvious—needs usually becomes less complicated by first determining what customers really seek in analyzing customer potentials and how to appeal to them. Of course, there is still a universe of diverse interests, which vary according to a number of factors, some of them inherent in the nature of the product. For example, in some products, safety is a prime consideration with a great many customers. At least one prominent manufacturer of microwave ovens lays great stress on the fact that the product has a most generous margin of safety from radiation, far in excess of that actually required.

There are many other factors that influence greatly the buying decisions of customers for manufactured products—overall quality, effectiveness, convenience, reliability, price, style, and so forth. The creator of goods to be sold must take such factors into account in designing and producing the items; for marketing, to be fully effective, cannot be an afterthought: It has to be a consideration when making decisions on what the enterprise is going to offer the customer prospect.

That means studying the market and learning what typical customer considerations are for the items contemplated. There are a few general considerations that will apply across the board in most (perhaps not all) cases. For example, there are in most lines of goods and industries two broad markets: the quality market and the low-price market. It is not possible to pursue both without making special preparations to do so (although it has been done frequently, with proper planning, and we will discuss that later). But there is always the customer whose first concern is quality, and with whom price is a secondary concern, not even to be discussed unless he or she is satisfied that the quality of the item is acceptable. Nonetheless, there is always that other customer whose first concern is price, and who is not interested in quality before ascertaining that the price is acceptable. Ergo, in most circumstances, the producer of goods must decide early whether to pursue the quality market or the low-price market.

Of course, the same considerations apply to the other factors. The entrepreneur must decide early on what factors are most likely to influence the customer or, conversely, what factors are to be built into the product and made the centerpiece of the marketing attack and sales appeal. Only on the basis of what it is likely to do for marketability of the item does it make good business sense to opt for a product offering convenience, durability, attractive style, or whatever are to be the major features. Almost always some compromise or trade-offs are required, and it is usually impossible to maximize one feature without reducing some other feature, such as quality versus price or style versus convenience. Probable success in the marketplace is the only really sound business reason for making these decisions.

SELLING GOODS CREATED
BY OTHERS

The considerations just presented for making decisions in connection with the creation of goods are the same *in principle* for organizing and operating a business devoted to selling the goods created by others. In practice, there are differences. The seller of goods manufactured by someone else has nothing to say about the features designed into the product, but must deal with the consequences, after the fact. That means that the seller of such goods has two broad options:

1. To organize marketing to sell to those customers for whom the goods you buy are designed and who are the best prospects for such goods.
2. To organize buying to order products most suitable to those classes of customers you wish to reach or feel most capable of reaching effectively.

You may not be entirely free to make this decision arbitrarily. It may be that you wish to handle a line of goods that entails protected territories or exclusive dealerships, and are unable to get the lines you want. Therefore, you may find yourself compelled to accept those lines you can get. In such a case, it is important that you gain a realistic look at who your best customer prospects are and pursue those prospects properly.

On the other hand, you may be deluding yourself as to what kinds of customer prospects you are in a good position to capture. Before venturing into a major commitment, you would do well to verify your market potential.

Selling goods, whether created by others or by yourself, usually occurs at two levels: wholesale and retail. Wholesale ordinarily means buying and warehousing the goods in quantity, reselling the goods to retailers in smaller quantities at a relatively modest markup or profit. Retailing is selling the goods to the consumer or end user, usually at a higher markup than the wholesaler gets.

Wholesaling is also done by organizations known as jobbers or distributors. (However, in some direct-response organizations, retailers are known as distributors.) Depending on the nature of the items and other circumstances, wholesalers may or may not have delivery services, and may or may not be within minutes of the retail establishments. For example, a wholesaler of heavy equipment is likely to have only one or two centrally located establishments and ship orders to retailers by common carriers; whereas the wholesaler of food products is compelled to warehouse his inventory in a location that permits daily delivery by his trucks, particularly if he handles perishable items.

There are many ways merchandise travels from its source—where it is created—to the ultimate consumer. There are, for a great many products, typical chains of descent from manufacturer to wholesaler to retailer to consumer, as depicted in Figure 1. There are also manufacturers who set up their own wholesale and retail operations (e.g., IBM), although they may operate each of these as separate organizations. And there are manufacturers who distribute their merchandise directly to dealers—retailers—such as Fuller Brush and Amway. These arrangements are illustrated in Figure 2.

Retailers may operate stores on well-traveled streets, doing their business across the counters of their retail establishments, or they may operate sales organizations, doing their business "on the street" through direct-sale campaigns. Or they may choose to reach and sell customers through other means, such as parties in the home (favored by some producers, such as Tupperware) or mail order catalogs, another widely practiced method for selling consumer goods.

In the case of Fuller Brush Company, the company distributes its products through some eight thousand to ten thousand salespeople-dealers. The Fuller Brush salesperson who appears at your door is an independent dealer, with an assigned territory. Founder Alfred C. Fuller began to recruit his dealers through want ads in newspapers, and was so successful that he continued the practice of recruiting through want ads ever since. Some companies, such as Amway, another producer of household products, use a variant of this, relying on a pyramid dealer network. Each dealer recruited may recruit subordinate dealers and turn some profit on sales of those subordinate dealers, who may, in turn, recruit other dealers. Of course, in the case of any pyramid, the system cannot go unchecked for long before those at the bottom of the pyramid become the victims of the system. However, legitimate pyramid plans, such as the Amway plan, make provision for newly recruited dealers to rise in the pyramid as they progress and succeed in recruiting others and making sales.

Different producers of products operate on different principles. Some who distribute their items through wholesaler and/or dealer networks exercise firm control and insist that their wholesalers and dealers follow company-prescribed plans and observe strict company rules in their marketing. Others permit their distributors and dealers a great deal of latitude to market the products as they see fit. For example, one producer may insist that dealers sell by house-to-house canvassing, establishing routes to be serviced regularly, while another producer may not care how you distribute the products as long as you sell enough volume to satisfy the company that you are doing justice to the territory you cover. However, those companies that have been successful in direct-selling through salespeople-dealers (e.g., Fuller Brush, Amway,

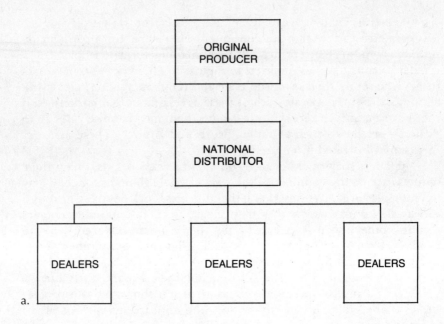

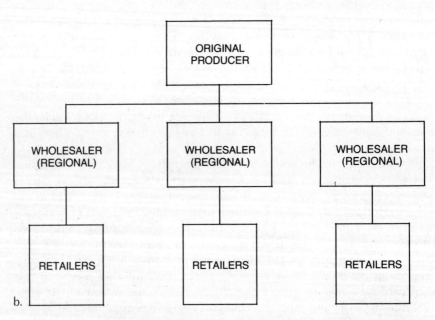

FIGURE 1. Typical distribution from producer through (a) a national distributor and (b) regional wholesalers.

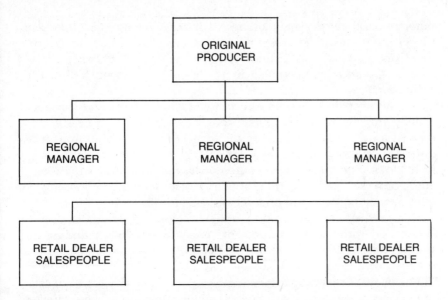

```
                    ┌─────────────┐
                    │  ORIGINAL   │
                    │  PRODUCER   │
                    └─────────────┘
         ┌─────────────────┼─────────────────┐
   ┌───────────┐     ┌───────────┐     ┌───────────┐
   │ REGIONAL  │     │ REGIONAL  │     │ REGIONAL  │
   │ MANAGER   │     │ MANAGER   │     │ MANAGER   │
   └───────────┘     └───────────┘     └───────────┘
         ┌─────────────────┼─────────────────┐
 ┌─────────────┐   ┌─────────────┐   ┌─────────────┐
 │ RETAIL DEALER│   │RETAIL DEALER│   │RETAIL DEALER│
 │ SALESPEOPLE │   │ SALESPEOPLE │   │ SALESPEOPLE │
 └─────────────┘   └─────────────┘   └─────────────┘
```

FIGURE 2. Direct-response marketing by appointing regional managers who supervise retail dealer-salespeople.

Avon) usually are reluctant to change their ways, for they don't want to tamper with success. And those who have been pursuing their systems successfully for many years usually are operating on the sound basis of experience and demonstrated long-term success, so it is probably advisable to heed what they say.

One essential difference between operating the retail store and selling through direct sales methods is this: Selling via the retail store is primarily passive. Although the retailer can advertise and create promotions, for the most part, the store is dependent on the incidence of walk-in customers—on traffic. The other approach—direct selling—is less passive, does not wait for the customer to walk in, but goes out knocking on doors. Each method has its pros and cons, which we will investigate and examine in a later chapter.

SELLING SERVICES

We are steadily becoming more and more of a service economy. That does not mean that eventually most of the economy will be devoted to selling services, but it does mean that the selling of services is becoming an ever more important part of the economy. To some degree this is the inevitable consequence of our burgeoning technology: The enormous and swift proliferation of computers mandated an equally swift and proliferating demand for related services—writing programs for com-

49

puters, operating and maintaining computer systems, and selling data-processing services. Other technology has created demands for services too. For example, the airlines require many services, as do many technological government agencies (Defense Department, NASA, EPA, and others).

The need for services affects the retail markets and businesses dealing directly with consumers, too. The electronics industry alone created a great many technological advances in household appliances, notably television, which spawned a large service industry. Growing technological developments in automobiles caused a great expansion of automotive services, and the popularity of home air-conditioning systems gave impetus to still another service industry.

There has been an almost parallel development of service needs in connection with social change. For one, the rapidly expanding and proliferating federal agencies have been the purchasers of billions of dollars worth of services, many of them highly technological or professional, many of them classed generally as consultant services. (The latter broad class of services to government agencies has alone been estimated to be a nine-billion-dollar annual market.)

Service-oriented enterprises then may be directed at serving the needs of individuals, organizations, or both. Of course, some of these services are inherently much more suited to one class of customers than to the other (that is, regarding individuals and organizations as two separate classes of customers). A television repair service is far more likely to get the bulk of its business from households than from organizations, while an educational design specialist is far more likely to do business with organizations.

Basically, services must usually be sold directly to the purchaser, inasmuch as one cannot usually package services and store them, waiting for customers to call, requesting them. Still, at least some services are sold through dealership arrangements of one sort or another. One such case is that of a service wherein one installs such devices as storm windows, bathtub and shower enclosures, and draperies. Quite often the sellers of such items do not have an in-house installation capability for the simple reason that it is not feasible economically to have an installer on the payroll. Instead, such dealers have made arrangements with a local installation contractor to take care of the dealer's installation needs. In some cases, it may be the customer who pays the installer directly; in other cases the installation contractor may collect fees from the dealer. In any case, installation contractors usually do work for a number of dealers—often for major stores such as Sears or Wards—and *their* customers may be either the buyers of the items being installed or the dealers, depending on the arrangements made and on general practices in the industry. For example, it is customary for the price of custom-made draperies to include installation, so the installer is working for the drapery dealer, who is the installer's customer. But it is customary in selling shower and bath enclosures to sell the unit to the customer, with installation costing extra. In this case, the dealer may collect from the customer and pay the installer, which means the dealer is still the customer; or the dealer may simply advise the buyer of the enclosure that an installer will be sent out and will collect from the buyer. In that case, the buyer is the installer's customer.

Thus, for any services arranged for through another party, either the other party may be the customer or the end user may be the customer, depending on how the service is brokered (that is, if it is passed to the installer as a convenience for the dealer's customer).

Marketing services should, of course, first consider whether the customers are going to be primarily organizations or individuals. A second consideration ought to be whether the typical customer's view of the service is going to be positive or negative. That is, does the service represent an unwanted expense caused by an unwanted occurrence, such as equipment failure? If so, the customer is likely to be somewhat negative, probably buying the service out of necessity and not with great enthusiasm. On the other hand, a service may be essentially positive— installing a new possession, for example—and may cause the customer to have a positive attitude.

Some services actually create a product the customer is eager to get—a resumé or business card, for example—and while the customer is buying a service, essentially, the customer judges the quality of the service by the quality of the end product. So, in the service business, we may also get into that ambiguous area in which it is not easily determined whether the customer is motivated to buy a service or a product. However, it has been my experience that when it comes to custom service, customers tend to judge and evaluate the end product by what they think of the service and the provider. That is, if the relationship with the customer is a happy one, the customer tends to be charitable in judging the quality of what is produced by the service; the reverse is also true—a less-than-pleasant relationship with the customer often leads to customer complaints about the product, although the product may in fact be quite well made.

This latter factor points up sharply a need touched on earlier: the need for customer confidence. This becomes a most important factor in many service businesses, especially when the service is a custom service and is performed on the customer's premises. As an excellent example of this, there was the case a few years ago of a TV serviceman sent out to repair a customer's set. After checking the receiver over carefully, the serviceman advised the customer that the chassis had to be removed to the shop for bench work. The customer objected and refused to allow the chassis to be removed. The customer insisted that the serviceman go back to his shop and send out the man who had serviced the woman's set several months previously. When the serviceman advised her that he was that same man, that this was his territory and only he covered it for his company, the woman snorted skeptically.

"You send that other fellow out," she insisted. "He knew what he was doing—" (because he had serviced the set in her home) "—but you don't know anything!"

She was quite sincere, but her judgment was distorted by her antipathy for anyone who proposed to remove her beloved TV from the house.

It's important to your marketing to recognize that emotional bias greatly affects human judgment: Hardly anyone is capable of being objective when stirred to some emotional state. Later, in discussing sales and advertising, we'll examine the question of emotion and objectivity in selling. However, it might well be noted that while customer confidence in the enterprise and entrepreneur is always important, it is of special importance when personal service is involved.

A FEW MISCELLANEOUS CONSIDERATIONS

For some types of business establishment, location is critically important. That is, it is quite often the principal determinant of success or failure in businesses that depend on customers visiting the establishment, such as with retail stores, restaurants, beauty salons, and other such enterprises. Again and again we see a succession of failures in the same location. One location near where this book is written, for example, has had three food establishments, none of which succeeded. The first was a major fast-food chain, the second was an independent fast-food enterprise, and the third was a sub and pizza shop, which also offered spaghetti and a few other Italian dishes. None have succeeded there, despite the fact that the building is located on a heavily traveled street in a crowded business district, with parking available on its own free lot. It *appears* to be a suitable location. Yet, careful study reveals its weaknesses, and experience verifies these: There is virtually no foot traffic here, although there is a steady stream of automobile traffic whizzing by all day. It is an inconvenient place to stop, and it is almost impossible to lure impulse patronage because one does not see the location well in advance of reaching it, and it would be quite dangerous to stop suddenly there. Even if it did not have these drawbacks, history is against it: Since two places already failed there, and one of them was an otherwise successful national chain, one would think it difficult to lure a third entrepreneur into trying the spot.

Restaurants are especially sensitive to location. You must first consider carefully what kinds of patrons you intend to appeal to, and then consider carefully whether the locations you are considering are suitable. In some cases, one type of restaurant may succeed where another has failed, simply because a location may be suitable to draw one type of patronage, but not another. For example, in industrial areas, peopled mostly by blue-collar workers, you often find virtual hordes of small family restaurants, almost cheek by jowl, yet surviving. You are unlikely to find the more pretentious and more expensive steak house or seafood emporium. On the other hand, tour an area close to a major airport and you will find an abundance of hotels and expensive restaurants designed expressly to attract travelers, especially those business executives who are armed with expense accounts. The Washington, D.C., suburbs, for example, have few of these modest little family restaurants because the area lacks the patronage for such places, although there is a relative abundance of fast-food palaces. For whatever reasons, the Washington suburbs are just not restaurant areas, as are the suburbs of many other cities. The failure rate of restaurant enterprises is always high everywhere, but it is an especially risky enterprise in the Washington area. That may be because the area in general is not heavily industrialized, and what industry is found in the area is such that the bulk of the employees are white-collar rather than blue-collar types. One possible reason for the rather unusual nature of the restaurant market in the area is the fact that by far a majority of the area residents are suburban dwellers with large mortgages; perhaps they choose to economize on eating out, as a result of carrying a heavy burden of housing cost. Nor are they a late-night crowd. Again and again entrepreneurs have opened restaurants and announced late-hour operations, only to begin closing much earlier after a few months of failing to get enough late-hour trade to justify staying open.

For one reason or another, different cities and different geographical areas each have their own customer characteristics. In Philadelphia you can't give away, much less sell, brown eggs; the public will buy only white eggs. But there are other areas where brown eggs are prized more highly than are white eggs. New York butchers cut meat a bit differently than do butchers in other cities, giving rise to the phrase "New York cuts," which are often offered elsewhere as prized portions. Certain dishes have their aficionados principally in certain locations—New York City has a great many Chinese fast-food places today, but I have not seen these in any other city.

Sometimes the characteristic is dictated by the location of the city.

A city close to the ocean or at the oceanside, for example, is certain to be a far better market for bathing and surfing accessories than would be a city in the Midwest. And a city in the heart of farm country is certainly a more likely location for the sale of farming implements than would be a town in coal-mining country.

Of course, these seem to be pretty obvious points to make, and yet small entrepreneurs (and even larger ones) often go blindly into a market without investigating the nature of the market, and are puzzled when their enterprises fail in short order. In the next chapter, we'll discuss some of this in more detail.

5

Where, When, How Marketing Begins

To be effective, marketing can never be an afterthought.

MARKETING BEGINS EARLIER THAN YOU THINK

By now you should have gotten a basic message in these pages: Marketing, as a function, begins when you first conceive a basic idea for a business. In other words, if you have not reasoned out in advance what you plan to sell and to whom you plan to sell, how can you possibly believe that you have a sound business idea or any probability of success? I have been constantly amazed by the number of entrepreneurs who write me to describe their marketing problems—their lack of success in marketing, to be more specific—and say such things as the following:

> trouble finding a match between my resource and the client's need.
> inability to locate good prospects for the services we offer.
> beginning to think I am not in the right field.
> mailed one thousand brochures with zero results.

Note some of these problems: At least three of these individuals started out with unclear ideas—perhaps no idea—of to whom they would make their offers and what needs their offers would promise to satisfy. Thomas Edison remarked once that inventing something was not nearly as difficult as deciding what needed to be invented. What he was saying, of course, was that it was futile to invent something for which there was no recognized need or, at the least, not enough recognized need to guarantee an adequate market.

55

The common mistake these entrepreneurs and many others make is this: they start their enterprises from the basis of what they believe they can do best, without due regard to the prospects they can reach and what those prospects are most likely to want to buy. Moreover, they make another all-too-common error of believing that fable about building a better mousetrap—that is, they sincerely believe that good marketing practice consists of telling prospects how good you are at what you do or how good your product is, and that prospects will then rush to buy. Anyone who has ever attempted to introduce a revolutionary new product or service knows better. If the new product or service is truly revolutionary—different from anything ever offered before—customers stay away in droves. If their curiosity is piqued, they stand and watch, waiting for "George" to buy and see if George gets stung or does well. That's why even legitimate businesses often find it beneficial to use shills—dummy customers who buy only to help prospects gain enough confidence in the product or service to become customers. That's why advertisers often use testimonials in their advertising, particularly if the testimonial comes from a public figure, such as a well-known entertainer or sports figure.

MOTIVATORS

Here we are approaching a most basic and critical subject in marketing and sales activity: how to motivate prospects to become customers, or what motivates prospects. Cynics say that the two most powerful motivators are fear and greed. All successful selling, according to this philosophy, results from persuading prospects that what the seller offers will either enrich the buyer or will enable the buyer to avoid some disaster. Although this is somewhat cynical and oversimplified, there is basic truth in it. Truly, all customers become customers because they believe that something desirable will result from the purchase, and that may well be simply avoidance of or better coping with some disaster. The most direct example of this is investment newsletters sold to those who believe that the investment advice contained therein will enrich them to at least some extent. But it is also possible to sell such newsletters by frightening the prospects, promising that the advice in the newsletter will enable them to avoid disastrous investments.

The first step is to decide which appeal to use (although it is possible to use both). Making the appeal is only one half the battle: You must also convince the prospect that you can and will deliver on your promise.

CONVINCERS

Convincing prospects is a follow-up to making the motivational appeal, and there are at least two variables:

1. Not everyone reasons the same way, so what you can say or do to convince one group of prospects may not work for another group.
2. What you must say or do to make your promises credible varies according to what you are promising, what it costs, how much risk the prospect takes, etc., in line with what you are offering.

Coping with the first problem is relatively simple. Most people cope with this simply by making several different kinds of explanations and providing different kinds of evidence—logic, testimonials, "authority," etc. It's the second consideration that requires the greatest amount of study and thought. Let's survey this a bit, to show how different the problem is for different situations.

First of all, there is a vast difference between offering a two-dollar product and a two-thousand-dollar product, or even a two-hundred-dollar product. Most people don't see enough risk in trying a two-dollar product or service to worry about it, and so they really do not need much convincing; they'll risk being wrong, for two dollars. Two hundred or two thousand dollars is an entirely different matter. Not many of us spend two hundred dollars or more casually. We need to be convinced that it's a sensible expenditure. So, a first consideration, in structuring appeals, is the size of the sale you are trying to make.

Another consideration is the nature of what you are offering for sale. If you are selling a well-known product, that has a great effect on how much convincing the prospect needs. But even "well-known" needs to be qualified. It is one thing to offer a food processor manufactured by one of our most famous manufacturers—General Electric, for example —and quite another to offer a food processor manufactured by someone most people have never heard of. Generically, the product may be well known, but if the manufacturer is not known to the prospect and the price is relatively high, you've got to compete with the other famous makers; it's name competition that must be overcome.

It's the same thing with services. It is likely that the owner of an RCA television set will accept the competence and dependability of an RCA service company's TV service without question, whereas that same TV owner probably would need some assurance before sending for Joe's Neighborhood TV Service.

This is even more true when professional services are involved—

medical, dental, legal, consulting, and others. In some cases, the cost involved is quite large; but even when it is not, there are other risk factors. The prospects are invariably rather cautious and require much assurance when selecting someone to provide the services. In many cases, prospects are reassured by the size of the seller—a large legal firm, with a lengthy list of law partners on the letterhead, or a large medical clinic may be accepted as evidence of quality and dependability. In other cases, prospects prefer to depend on the recommendation of a friend or relative. There are even circumstances where the recommendation of strangers is accepted. For example, an individual needing legal services for the first time might call the local bar association and ask for help, or he or she might ask a neighbor.

Some of the influences that motivate a prospect to become a customer—or not to—are quite subtle, and must be understood by the seller. Beginners in consulting, for example, are usually baffled when the cards, brochures, and sales letters they send out do not bring back orders or even invitations to call and discuss their services. What they fail to grasp is the basic difficulty in motivating prospects to agree to spend relatively large sums of money—consulting fees—for the counsel of a stranger. When you go to a doctor or dentist, even if he or she is a complete stranger, you have at least the assurance that the doctor or dentist has the proper degrees and is licensed to do whatever it is he or she does. When you engage the services of a consultant, you usually do not have any such assurance, but are taking the consultant at face value. To sell consulting services effectively, the consultant must do whatever is necessary to provide evidence of capability and dependability.

Even location is a part of this. When a building becomes known as a professional building or a medical building, that alone confers a certain degree of respectability and credibility on all those practicing there. And even in other kinds of enterprises, location often has an important bearing on marketing success.

SELECTING THE RIGHT LOCATION IS PART OF MARKETING

In some enterprises, location is everything. Restaurants are a good example of this. If you propose to open a fancy dinner restaurant in the financial district of your city, you are forgetting the fact that financial districts are pretty much deserted by 5:30 P.M. You could do a lunch and probably a breakfast business in a financial district, but you'd have a most difficult time doing a dinner business there.

On the other hand, such a restaurant would not go well in the industrial district, either. In some cases, industrial districts are also deserted by early evening. In any case, you are not likely to find the kind of patrons you want in the industrial district.

Suppose that you know of an available location along the waterfront in your city, close by the docks, where ships are loaded and unloaded constantly. Would that be a good spot for a fancy dinner restaurant?

Surprisingly enough, it might well be, especially if you are contemplating a seafood restaurant. Frequently, locating a seafood restaurant in such a spot adds to its appeal, and patrons will go out of their way to have dinner there—provided your food is satisfying to them.

This may seem like a violation of the basic rule about locating your establishment to attract the kind of patrons your plan dictates you must attract, but in truth it is not. In the restaurant business, particularly where dinner restaurants are concerned, people love atmosphere, and locating a seafood restaurant in a waterfront area, or decorating a steak house with rustic fixtures, encourages patrons to believe that the cuisine is going to be authentically whatever the house purports to specialize in. In fact, with a bit of luck and a bit of clever marketing promotion, you may well make your establishment a local "in place." This lures patrons even when your restaurant is somewhat inconvenient for them to reach.

Sometimes liabilities can be turned into assets. Or, to put this into a slightly different light, what might be a liability in other circumstances may be an asset if it is planned so. For example, there are cases where an inconvenient location is actually an asset, luring customers far more effectively than would a location convenient for them. Many successful discount outlets have been based in completely out-of-the-way sites, which helped to draw patrons because it lent great credibility to the discount claim.

Today's customers are quite a bit more sophisticated and more knowledgeable than were typical customers of a half-century ago. This is the result of movies, TV, travel, and other conditions of modern life. There are no rubes left, at least not in the sense of years ago, when farmers and people from small towns often had never been more than a dozen miles from home, and had no notion of "city ways." Today's customer is educated enough and sophisticated enough to be somewhat suspicious of bargains and extravagant claims. If you hope to convince today's customers that you offer more than your competitors, you had better be prepared to furnish some pretty good evidence.

Robert Hall furnished that evidence with constant repetition of the "plain pipe rack" argument, although they finally ran out of marketing steam and succumbed to competition. But there are many establishments today who still thrive on the "walk three flights and save a bundle" sales argument. If you drive around eastern Pennsylvania, anywhere in the vicinity of Reading, York, Lancaster, or other nearby towns, you'll find that discount stores have billboard advertising and brochures scattered everywhere, directing you to their special, out-of-the-way locations. To many of the patrons of these places, the out-of-the-way location is itself a draw for at least two reasons: For one, it lends credibility to the discount claim and makes the customer reasonably confident that shopping there means saving money and being quite shrewd—an appeal to the ego; second, finding these places is itself fun for many of these customers, something of an adventure.

There are cases of an entrepreneur launching an enterprise—perhaps a retail store—that does not succeed, but which the entrepreneur sometimes salvages with a sharp change of direction. When Charles Aronson started his machine shop in Arcade, New York, he wasn't absolutely sure what he would be manufacturing in that shop, but he started with the idea of producing fixture blocks of an advanced design, which he had conceived and perfected. Certain circumstances made this plan impossible to pursue, and Aronson was forced to turn to other things. Due to his own unusual abilities to improvise brilliantly and to adapt swiftly to circumstances, Aronson was able to produce a number of different products successfully before he finally settled on a complete line of welding positioners. Few entrepreneurs could survive under those circumstances—most small businesses do not have the financial resources, nor do their owners have the other necessary resources of personal strength necessary to survive an initial setback. For most small entrepreneurs, it is absolutely necessary to get it right the first time. Hence, it is essential to do accurate marketing research and make valid marketing decisions up front, before making final commitments. Let's consider, then, the three basics of marketing studies which are the vital ingredients: what you will sell, to whom you will sell it, and how you will reach those to whom you propose to sell.

WHAT, TO WHOM, AND HOW YOU WILL SELL

A great many individuals choose to retire or enter into semiretirement in southern Florida, especially in the Fort Lauderdale-Miami area. And a great many of these retirees have been successful business people elsewhere and do not wish to be completely idle, so they invest their money in some enterprise which will occupy their time and provide a business challenge. Since many have spent as many as thirty or forty years building their modest fortunes in some business elsewhere in the country, they are quite bored with that business and want to adventure into something different. In one case, two fellows, whom we'll call Bert and Joe, sold out an automobile repair establishment they had operated successfully in Brooklyn for many years, and decided to enjoy the sunshine of Miami Beach. These two gentlemen invested their capital in a plant that manufactured concrete blocks, for which there was an eager market in southern Florida, since there is no clay there from which to make bricks, and no natural stone, either. In fact, quarrying for aggregate for concrete mixing consists of digging canals with draglines to get at the coral substrata: Coral and sand are the only locally available materials for aggregate.

Since construction, especially of private homes, was in a boom stage in southern Florida, as it had been for years, manufacturing concrete block seemed a sound enough proposition. Neither Bert nor Joe really knew anything about the construction or the builder's supply businesses, and they soon found themselves operating at such a loss that they were forced to sell out for whatever they could get. The losses were such that Bert and Joe had to go back to what they knew: automobile repair. So at their relatively advanced ages, Bert and Joe started another automobile-repair business.

The story is not an isolated one. It has been repeated again and again, and there is a moral in it: Stick with what you know. The other fellow's business may appear to be an easy one to run, but it probably is not. The point of this is to consider what you know best and are best suited to, in deciding what you are going to sell.

There are several different aspects to related experience and know-how, all of which are important in different ways. First, there is *technical knowledge*—knowing how to make the product or perform the service. There is also *market knowledge*—defining who needs the product or service and why it is needed. There is *selling knowledge*—conveying what induces prospects to buy the product or service. And there is *competitor knowledge*—being aware of those already established in the field with products or services, and what their relative strengths and weaknesses are.

All of this information is needed and must be considered when deciding what you are going to sell. So the process, overall, is necessarily an iterative, or repetitive, one. That is, you start with a tentative decision to sell some product or service—at least, the decision ought to be tentative until you have cranked in the other factors. Ultimately, you will arrive at final decisions. Figure 3 illustrates the concept in broad terms. First you arrive at a basic idea of what you will sell. Then you consider carefully to whom you will sell, and then how you will get your offers presented to those whom you propose to make customers. Each step, however, is a reason to go back and look at earlier steps, to reevaluate them. For example, it is futile to decide that you will sell to a target population you can't reach, obviously, but how often a business has been launched without considering whether the operator of the business could do what he so blithely assumed he could do! Let's consider a hypothetical case to illustrate this more fully.

Feedback information to modify earlier decisions.

FIGURE 3. Basic steps in initial interaction.

You decide that there is a dire need for information on financial management: Few small companies really understand financial management, and in these days of tight money and high interest rates, the lack of such expertise can easily be fatal to small businesses. You yourself are quite expert in this field: You know where and how to raise funds to back operations; how to do so at least risk, lowest costs, and best terms generally; how to maximize cash flow in the company by such methods as minimizing overdue accounts; and many other aspects of financial management usually known only to specialists in that field, and not commonly known to the average CPA or company comptroller.

There is really no question in your mind that there is a need for this know-how, that it would be quite valuable to many, if not most, small companies who are not in a position to have a full-time expert at this on their own staffs. Nor is there any question in your mind that you have the know-how and can impart it to others. So that first box in Figure 3 you mentally label FINANCIAL MANAGEMENT SERVICE. At this point, you have not yet decided what you mean by *service*. Does it mean actually doing financial management on a contractual or fee basis? Acting as a consultant? Contractor? Or will you train the client's staff? Sell them a manual you have written? Give them a computer program? Some combination of all these?

Let's shelve that question for the moment and go on. The next box we want to focus on is the one that tells us who our intended customers are: Who needs what we plan to offer? Company presidents? Comptrollers? Vice-presidents of companies? And what kinds of companies? Manufacturers? Distributors? Service companies? Construction contractors? The answer to what kinds of companies is probably those whose business is such that they are compelled to carry a large number of receivables and therefore keep a great deal of capital tied up.

And what's the best way to reach those prospects after we have decided what to offer and to whom to offer it? Mail? Salesmen on the street? Advertisements to develop leads? Telephone solicitation? And if by mail, where/how do we get suitable mailing lists? If by advertising, where do we advertise?

By now it's quite apparent that it will not be easy to make all these decisions. Certainly, it would be foolish to make them arbitrarily. We've no way to know yet whether the prospects will agree that they need such help badly enough that we will be able to induce them to pay for it. Even if they agree that they need such help and are willing to buy it, how much will they spend? Will they be willing to have some of their staffs attend training courses, or would they prefer to buy consulting services? And if consulting services, will they agree to an annual contract for ongoing services, or will they be willing to buy only a one-time consulting effort to design and install a system for them to run—a turnkey operation? Which kinds of companies are likely to be most responsive? Will we do best to offer alternatives and let the prospect select the kind of service most attractive to him? Would different kinds of companies want different kinds of services?

Typically, the new entrepreneur goes into such planning with a mind already prejudiced by 1) past experience or 2) personal preferences. That is, if the planner has been working for a company that was highly successful in selling financial consulting services, the new entrepreneur is likely to opt for this without further thought, convinced that this method works and that there is a proven market for such a service. (That's following John D. Rockefeller's advice to emulate established success, of course.) Or, if the entrepreneur happens to like lecturing and feels quite secure doing so, he or she is most likely to opt without further ado for offering training programs or seminars in financial management. Only later will the entrepreneur discover whether that early decision was a good or bad one, and that knowledge may come only after disastrous experience.

Of course, one cannot know everything in advance; no amount of advance analysis, research, investigation, and planning can take the place of actual operating experience. A gentleman who began a newsletter service in Washington, D.C., soon learned that while the newsletter service was viable enough, the seminar business was far more promising. Today, his newsletter business goes on, but the bulk of his energies and efforts go into his four-million-dollar-a-year seminar enterprises.

Still, market research and planning ought to begin before business decisions are final—they are, in fact, part of the general planning. The example of the preceding paragraphs should demonstrate that deciding the questions of what you will sell, to whom you will sell it, and how you will reach those to whom you propose to sell are not independent of or unrelated to each other. Quite the contrary—they are closely related. You can only sell something for which there is a need. You can sell that something only to those who have that particular need. And you can sell to those prospects only if you can somehow make your offer known to them. To be successful, you must be able to satisfy that need at a price the customer is willing to pay, for one thing. And there has to be a large enough market—enough prospects who have the need—to make the whole idea viable.

THE QUESTION OF COMPETITION

You should not launch your enterprise without considering the competition. First of all, is your competition direct or indirect? Here is what that means:

If you are marketing a product or service quite similar to something else being marketed, you are marketing against direct competition. But there is sometimes indirect competition, too. That's a product or service that is different from what you offer, but which accomplishes the same thing generally or is in pursuit of the same dollars. For example, two sellers of electric blenders are in direct competition, but a seller of electric blenders is indirectly competing with a seller of food processors: The food processor is a different machine, but it can do the same things that a blender can do. A customer is less likely to buy a blender if he or she has bought a food processor. In another sense, every business is in indirect competition, at least, with every other business that pursues the same class of customers, because all are competing for a limited number of dollars. The customer who buys new shoes on Saturday night will probably not buy a new overcoat on that same night. The merchants selling these items are competing with each other for the customer's dollars, despite the fact that they sell goods to satisfy different kinds of needs.

The entrepreneur who comes up with a truly new idea has no direct competition, and tends to see this as a great advantage. Not so; it's far more likely to be a disadvantage. It's rarely easy to succeed with something new—the customer will tend to resist strongly that which is new because it's also strange. The customer is not sure if this new product or service is any good, if it will do what the seller claims, if it's worth the price being asked, and perhaps even is skeptical about whether it satisfies a need. In most cases, introducing something new involves special problems, which we'll discuss in detail in a later chapter.

In any case, before making your final decision, consider the competition. How much competition is there? How firmly is it established? Is there one competitor who is clearly the leader in the field, who perhaps actually dominates the field? Is that competitor vulnerable in any way you can exploit? Can you underprice the competition? Give better service? Deliver more rapidly?

Although Remington Rand was the first company to market an electronic computer, IBM soon took the lead and still leads the field today by a wide margin. IBM became so firmly entrenched in the computer field that even such giants as RCA and GE withdrew from the field, licking their wounds, after losing a great deal of money. That is not to say that no one can survive against big-league competition; Control Data Corporation, Honeywell, and Burroughs Corporation have managed to remain in the computer business, but firmly entrenched competition is something to consider soberly before making a commitment. On the other hand, if you can cut out some special segment of the market where the leader is not particularly strong or which the leader has not pursued very enthusiastically, you may have an entirely different ball game. In the computer business, this is what Apple has done, specializing in small computers.

That is an excellent way to analyze a market for its potential. Rarely does any company, even the largest supercorporation, do everything well. If you can find some slice of the market that no one is paying a great deal of attention to, and you believe there is the potential to build a sizable business by specializing in what that market slice needs, then you needn't worry about competition, but only about how to pursue that portion of the market.

However, there is at least one huge advantage in entering the lists against well-established and successful competitors: They have already created the market and have made consumers conscious of the need for the product; they have also developed demand through their advertising and other marketing activities. Apple Computers could probably never have succeeded in what they are now doing had they attempted it twenty years ago, before the market for computers was as well established as it is today. Giants like IBM and others broke the ground, doing the advertising and sales promotion, creating the acceptance of and ultimately the demand for computers, so that Apple did not meet much sales resistance when they came along with their small computers.

In some situations, the small business can prosper from the crumbs falling off the big competitor's table. A small shoe store, a few doors from a large department store, will get at least some overflow business—customers who are unwilling to tolerate the generally less personal service one gets in the superstore, or are unwilling to wait to get any service at all. This is true in all industries. Even in such industries as computers and other large and costly equipment, if you can deliver more rapidly than the bigger companies, you can capture a certain amount of the business simply by accommodating those customers who want faster delivery than they can get from large companies. This is certainly a factor to consider when evaluating the market and estimating what market share you are likely to be able to capture.

Don't be misled by appearances. A competitor who appears to be well entrenched with a large market share may not be well entrenched at all: He may have a great many unhappy customers who would be glad to change suppliers, given a good opportunity to do so. It's not unusual for a company to become "fat, dumb, and happy" when they have prospered and when there seem to be no serious challengers anywhere in sight. Sometimes such a company becomes careless, even arrogant, in handling customers. Don't guess; check. Do your research. Talk to people. Ask questions. Count the traffic.

In one such case, a large company bought out a smaller one which had held a large and profitable government contract for years. The new management was, of course, happy to take over the lucrative contract. However, after only a few years, the company became careless and began to treat the federal agency's executives with contempt. The word trickled out that the government agency was most unhappy with their contractor, and would award the contract to anyone else who came along with a good proposal when the contract came up for renewal, and they did so. The successful bidder for the contract had been tuned in to the scuttlebutt, knew that they stood an excellent chance of winning the contract, and were thus encouraged to go up against the much larger competitor in pursuing it.

A brochure published by the Small Business Administration on the subject of marketing makes the point that some marketing research is nothing but garbage. This is not a condemnation of anything; it means that valuable marketing information can be gained by searching through garbage! For example, a mail-order dealer I know makes it a practice to sift through the trash barrel at his post office occasionally, retrieving advertising literature patrons have thrown away. He takes this to his office to study, and the studies he makes tell him several things immediately.

By sorting out the trash into various categories—the ones that have been opened and discarded, those that were discarded without being opened, and those that were opened but not unfolded and, presumably, not read. By accumulating enough examples of each of these categories, you can begin to see the patterns. You can begin to gauge what kinds of offers appeal to respondents and what kind of copy induces them to open envelopes that are obviously advertising solicitations. You can learn a great deal about writing copy and structuring promotions that do work. Most significant of all, if you have read the opinions of those who write knowledgeably about advertising and marketing promotions, you will begin to check up on such advice and find out how well it works—or doesn't work.

Trash barrels also yield up used containers, indicators of what people have been buying. For example, if you attend some sort of fair or other function where there are hordes of people, and you are interested in which of several competing refreshment stands are doing the greatest volume, even a casual inspection of the trash barrels will furnish good clues. If you are attending a trade show or convention with an exhibit floor, walk around and have a look at which booths are running out of literature and which have apparently untouched stacks on their tables. Here too, note which kinds of literature populate the trash barrels most generously.

The American Marketing Association identifies marketing research as "the systematic gathering, recording, and analyzing of data about problems relating to the marketing of goods and services." That definition does not say as much as it ought to, of course, because it really does not say much at all. It's a typical academic phrase, and avoids the heart of the problem, which varies slightly depending on which of these situations you are in when conducting or planning to conduct market research:

1. Contemplating an enterprise already decided on, at least tentatively.
2. Contemplating an enterprise, but still considering various approaches and not settled firmly on what to sell or how to sell it.
3. Already established in an enterprise and trying to improve sales volume.
4. Doing preliminary study to determine whether there is a viable approach to starting an enterprise in anything suitable to your own circumstances.

The differences in your marketing research for each of these situations are highly significant. In each case, you are dealing in learning something about the preferences of people. Marketing research is definitely oriented to people and their behaviors as related to buying: what they buy or are likely to buy, how they buy, why they buy, how much they will spend, and so forth. However, in one case you are researching what people are doing currently, while in another case you are trying to determine what they are likely to do. In still a third case you may be trying to determine how behaviors are changing, or trying to identify a particular market segment that does or doesn't buy a given product or type of product.

In market research, as in many other human activities, problems arise because we attempt to do something under as vague a definition as that cited above. In fact, if you do attempt to gather and analyze all the "data about problems relating to the marketing of goods and services," you will undertake an impossible job because you won't know where you are headed—what your specific objective is. Unfortunately, too often, we do exactly this—start out to do something without a specific, defined objective. This means that we start out to do something without knowing exactly what we are trying to do! It is an absolute essential in marketing that we *decide exactly what we need to know before we begin.* The reliability of our results is almost certain to depend on two factors: how narrowly focused our objective is and how well we have defined our objective before beginning. You have little chance of getting useful results if you start out with an objective as broad as trying to determine what consumer product sells best in mail order. That's far too general to be useful. You must select a specific item or class of items being sold by mail and direct your marketing research to evaluating that market. Or, you might attempt to compare the sales of some specific item or class of items with another specific item or class of items. Even then, you have to decide how to address this objective—specifically, what data do you want? Number of orders? Volume in dollars? If dollars, retail dollars, wholesale dollars, or profit dollars? And to be really useful, you probably want to stratify the data by seasonal patterns: What are the typical figures for the various times of year? Also, where do the items sell best? Most poorly? What kinds of buyers account for the largest part of the sales volume? Which for the smallest part?

As you can see, to be really useful, the research must answer a great many such questions. Otherwise you might select an excellent item, invest a great deal of money to set up a first-class sales organization, armed with fine literature and excellent advertising—and fail completely because you addressed the wrong market or made some other fundamental mistake.

Marketing research is the second step in launching any kind of enterprise after first deciding to launch an enterprise or to do some research in preparation for it. It's true enough that hunches pay off for many entrepreneurs, and many entrepreneurs start a business in a field in which they are already quite expert as a result of prior experience. As an employee of a company, you may have learned your own field so well and diagnosed a need so accurately that you can launch straightaway into a successful venture. But, of course, you already have done your marketing research; you've been doing it for a long time as an inevitable consequence of your employment experience. If you are fortunate enough to have the right information before you launch your new enterprise, you need not mount an unnecessary marketing study of any kind. But don't deceive yourself: Many experienced people quit their jobs to spin off a new enterprise, sure that they understand the market and the industry well enough, and discover that they do not know how to market. By far the most common failure is that of identifying prospects and needs and relating them to what they have to offer. They make the mistake of beginning their reasoning with what they have to offer or wish to offer, rather than trying to determine what there is a need for and then matching what they can offer with what that need is.

Most of us cannot sit down and reason all of this out. It happens that way rarely, fictional success stories to the contrary. The fact is that almost all business success is a result of trial and error. It begins with certain assumptions or premises, and succeeds when the entrepreneur is wise enough to check constantly and modify plans constantly as experience reveals what was true and what was untrue about those early assumptions and how they should be changed to agree with reality. Let's look now at a few case histories that illustrate this.

6

The Market Analysis

Market analysis is getting down to the heart of people's needs and wants, and this is the most basic of keys to business success.

WHAT ARE YOU OFFERING?

You will recall that *understanding your business means seeing it from the customer's viewpoint*—specifically, what it is that the customer wants to realize as a benefit in buying from you. To identify this in terms useful for marketing, you must learn to think differently. You must learn to *sell the satisfaction of needs*, rather than products and services per se. For example, I mistakenly offered information about the government market when I began to publish a newsletter called *Government Marketing News*. After a long period of struggle, subsidizing a newsletter that did not pay its own way, I began to learn how to sell help in winning government contracts, instead of news items and other information. At first I thought I was in the newsletter publishing business, selling newsletters to my customers. Later I decided that I was in the information business, giving my customers useful information. Ultimately, I learned that subscriptions came more abundantly when I discovered that I was in the business of helping people win government contracts. The companies receiving my advertising literature did not want information; they wanted contracts.

Perhaps this appears to be a subtle consideration, especially since customers do not consciously say to themselves, "I don't want to buy a newsletter or information; I want to buy help in winning contracts." Subtle or not, unless you think in these terms, you will fail to give your prospects the most compelling reasons to buy from you. Your appeals will not be as sharply focused on benefits as they ought to be.

Of course, when we talk about getting orders, we are talking sales, rather than marketing. No matter; marketing should provide the analyses, decide what the customer needs are and how to appeal to them most effectively. Once having determined what those needs or wants are, it is a proper marketing function to modify the product or service so as to respond more effectively to that need.

STRUCTURING THE OFFER TO THE NEED

In the case of my newsletter, it was quite easy to modify it once I came to an accurate realization of what the customer wanted. I simply began to feature more coverage on tips and other help in winning contracts. I made this a major consideration in deciding what would go into the news-letter every month. It's not as easy to do this when you are dealing in a product created by someone else. For example, if you are retailing manufactured goods you have no choice but to sell the goods as they come to you and to use such counter displays and other promotional aids as are supplied by the manufacturers. However, there are a number of reasons for customers patronizing you rather than one of your compet-itors. Remember that you are not selling the products, you are selling things such as convenience, confidence, ego gratification, and even friendship. Let me illustrate this with a personal example:

In these days of supermarkets and chain stores, most of us have come to accept thoroughly impersonal relationships with clerks, a minimum of service, and even a degree of indifference on the part of those with whom we transact business. I, for one, remembering different days (the thirties), thoroughly dislike this, and will invariably patronize the small, individually owned business, if the proprietor goes to the trouble of making me feel welcome. I patronize one store, where the proprietor has known my name since the first time I entered his place of business. He has never failed since to give me a friendly greeting and offer to help me find what I'm looking for, cash my checks, or help in whatever way I might possibly need help. I often go out of my way to patronize that place because shopping there is such a pleasant experi-ence. That merchant isn't selling me merchandise (which I could get almost anywhere, sometimes at lower prices) nearly as much as he is selling me a pleasant social encounter.

WHAT DO MOST PEOPLE WANT?

The basic needs that all of us have to some degree are love, security, prestige, recognition, and ego gratification. Or are these all part of the need for security? It appears to me that almost all human needs relate to the need for security. We want to be loved, we want to be liked, we want to have enough money, we want to be warm, we want to be well fed, we want to laugh, we want companionship. But, if you examine them closely enough, perhaps you'll come to agree that all of these are elements contributing to a sense of security. What most of us need or think we need may not in actuality be security or any part of security, but if it imparts a *sense* of security, it serves the same purpose. We ought to recognize that the most basic human need is the need to feel secure.

WHAT IS SECURITY?

There is no such thing as absolute security, and few of us are willing to pay the price for even approaching such a goal. Probably military service imparts a satisfying feeling of security to career military people, and we know that prisoners often become "institutionalized," which means that they are totally uncomfortable outside the penal institution. These are the extreme cases, but even here, there are elements lacking that most of us need as part of feeling secure.

Security means a reliable satisfying of all needs, physical and emotional. The individual has a need for food, warmth, clothing, sleep, and a few other physical requirements. Most of us also have an emotional need for companionship, laughter, being liked, being loved, and being respected; we have inner drives impelling us to try to achieve these things. But those drives vary a great deal in different individuals: Some have intense needs for prestige—ego gratification—for example, while others do not. In the business world, there are those who prefer title and relative position in an organization to money, and they will cling to a low-paying job rather than take a better-paying job that offers no prestige within the organization. To those individuals, their titles and local prestige—their *positions*—represent security.

That explains why advertisements appealing to a man's desire to be macho work well, at least with respect to those who feel the need to be what we used to call he-men. Some men place great importance on an active love life, and are highly motivated by commercials that sell such items as after-shave lotions with the promise that they vastly increase sex appeal. Sellers of men's clothing often suggest in their advertisements that the three-piece suit is a milestone on the route to career success.

On the other hand, fear of consequences may be used instead of the promise of some highly desirable benefit. The promise is that the customer can avoid an unwelcome fate by buying whatever the advertiser is selling. Obviously, all insurance and safety devices are often sold exactly this way. The implication is that (1) the prospect cannot afford to risk being without the protection offered by the product or service, and (2) no competing product offers as much or as reliable a freedom from danger. There is considerable evidence that fear is a highly effective motivator, possibly more effective than the promise of great rewards.

These are times when we have many forces working to instill a sense of guilt in us. So guilt is used effectively as a sales motivator too. Insurance companies often use guilt, broadly suggesting that we are falling down in our responsibilities as parents, spouses, and citizens if we have not provided for our loved ones by signing up. Thus, the sense of security includes freedom from fear, and that includes the fear of being guilty.

If we consider the ways in which we can contribute to our customer's sense of security, we have identified something we can probably sell. If it can be made part of the actual product or service sold, or in some way built into the enterprise, it is all to the good.

THE DATA YOU WANT TO GATHER

In making a typical market analysis, these are the questions to which you must seek answers:

- Who are my customers or potential customers?
- What are their characteristics?
- Where do they live? Work?
- What do they ordinarily buy? What don't they buy?
- Are they now buying something competitive?
- Can I be competitive in prices?
- How much of the market does my chief competitor have?
- What methods are my competitors using? TV spots? Direct mail? Radio spots? Newspaper ads? Telephone book ads? Sales? Circulars? Tie-ins with other merchants?
- What are my competitors' weaknesses? Poor service? Surly clerks? Inadequate stock? Sloppy store displays? No return or guarantee policy?
- What do customers think of my competitors?

GATHERING THE DATA

Determining who your customers are—or who they will be—is something you must do by identifying what needs your product or service satisfies. Of course, the nature of what you offer dictates at least some customer characteristics automatically. For example, if you sell cosmetics, it is possible that you will do some business with husbands and boyfriends buying presents, but the bulk of your business must be with women. (Perhaps you could increase your business by a significant percentage if you did something to make men feel at home in your establishment. Maybe you should consider a service designed especially to help men select cosmetics for their wives and girl friends.)

Location is necessarily a factor in who your customers are, because to some extent it dictates what kinds of people you will have to draw your customers from. If you are in a downtown business district primarily occupied by office buildings, your pool of prospects is likely to consist of office workers, and a large percentage of those will be young, single women. If you are downtown, in a location where there are many other shops, you will get shoppers in general to draw from. If there are a number of exclusive shops in the area, you will get a goodly percentage of shoppers who are wealthy enough to indulge their tastes for exclusive items.

According to these factors, you decide what needs you will appeal to. For the wealthy shopper who patronizes only the exclusive shops, you will have to appeal to that need to feel that the customer is buying merchandise a cut or two above that sold in other emporiums. Young office workers, if they are single, probably worry about their sex appeal; they want to be not only in style, but attractive to the men and women around them. They have the ego need to feel attractive.

What your customers buy is something you usually learn only through experience. Unless the merchandise you buy may be returned for credit, you buy cautiously at the outset, until you learn what your customers want and do not want. You may be able to get an advance idea about this by shopping other stores in the area and seeing what they carry and what appears to move well. Also, you can ask the local wholesalers; they know what will move and what does not move in each location.

There are some enterprises where you have only a handful of competitors—possibly even as few as one or two. In such a case, the questions of who dominates the market, to what degree, how firmly the competitor is entrenched, what share of the market you can hope for, and whether that share will enable you to survive become important questions. Where the market is shared by a great many competitors, as is the case with retail shops, location becomes the more important question.

In any case, you'll want to study the marketing methods competitors use. It's not difficult to determine what marketing methods are in use; they're pretty obvious. How successful those methods are is a bit more difficult to determine, but there are ways to get a general idea of whether the various methods are marginal, highly successful, or totally unsuccessful. One way to do this is to study the history of each method.

Any method that has been used repeatedly is certainly working, or the entrepreneur would have abandoned it long ago. Conversely, any methods used once or twice and then abandoned almost surely will not work well for you.

This information is the hardest to gather. Frequently, you get such data only from your own customers who happen to be former customers of your competitors. But you can have relatives and friends shop your competitors and make judgments as to what is good, bad, strong, and weak about competitive enterprises.

On the other hand, for a typical retail-store enterprise in which you handle lines of goods available in many other stores, what competitors do may be of little importance to you. Often, success depends entirely on what you do and not at all on what competitors do. In such cases, concentrate entirely on what you must do to create traffic in your establishment and to satisfy your customers.

This analysis and data gathering was based on the hypothesis of a retail sales operation offering established products already well known by type of product, if not by brand name. Obversely, there are lines of merchandise in which hardly any consumer is familiar with brand names. For example, customers rarely ask to see furniture or clothing by brand names. Whether customers know the products best by brand names or by generic names, the products are well established, and customers need not be educated to an appreciation of what the product does. For this reason, it has long been my custom to refer to such well-known products (whether well known by brand or by generic name) as commodities, and I will continue the practice here. Products that are not commodities are those products requiring the customer to be especially educated. Teflon-coated pots and pans were sold by in-store demonstrations to educate the consumers; food processors were introduced to the public in the same way.

The same philosophy applies to services. One need not educate the public to radio and TV repair services, nor to automobile repairs, but if you have developed a new treatment which you believe will grow hair, you will probably have to work at explaining the process before you'll persuade patrons to buy it. Such services are commodity services, thus distinguishing them from such services as the recovery of lost golf balls or the conversion of your TV into a computer.

WHERE DOES MARKET ANALYSIS TAKE YOU?

Because market analysis is more art than science, it should be creative. Analysis is not an end in itself. Its purpose is to gather data with which *to do something:*

1. Use it to set up your enterprise or modify your enterprise in such a manner that it emulates success models.
2. Use it as a basis for synthesizing new approaches, to do things differently and more successfully than others.

Let's consider that second idea, in which we actually go from analysis to synthesis—formulation of something new, based on what we have learned.

Synthesizing is creating, and we have talked earlier about creativity —what it is, what its elements are, how it works. Creativity is not ordinarily a logical process, although logic enters into it at some point. As we saw earlier, the subconscious mind usually provides the basic inspiration for the creative idea, and it rarely comes when you are concentrating on the problem and trying consciously to find the answer. It is far more likely to occur after you have done a great deal of conscious concentration on the problem, and then put it to rest to go on to other pursuits. The "inspiration" generally makes itself known when you are relaxing in some manner.

In this case, what we should be striving for is an extrapolation of the data we gathered earlier to see what other marketing methods we might employ. That attack might address any or all of the following:

1. New and different uses for the product or service.
2. New and different users for the product or service.
3. New and different distribution methods.
4. New and different sales arguments or promotions.

A miner in Minnesota, Carl Wickman, opened an agency to sell Hupmobiles, an automobile of prewar vintage. He found sales rather slow and searched about for customer needs in the area. He soon discovered that most of the miners working in the famed Mesabi iron ore range lacked transportation to get to their jobs every day. After raising six hundred dollars by taking in a partner, Wickman started a transportation service between Hibbing and Alice, over a four-mile, unpaved stretch of primitive road. He started the service with a seven-passenger Hupmobile, charging passengers fifteen cents one way or twenty-five cents round trip. Sometimes he carried extra passengers clinging to the running boards and fenders of the vehicle, which Wickman had "stretched" to accommodate ten passengers seated inside. Thus was born the industry that today is dominated by Greyhound bus, and which supports several other sizable bus companies.

John H. Patterson became an innovator through desperate necessity. He had bought out a failing manufacturer of cash registers, then crude and unfamiliar devices. Learning how stubborn was the sales resistance to this new product, he tried to get out from under it, but could not; so he set his jaw and vowed to make a success of this company, which he renamed the National Cash Register Company. Making that vow good compelled Patterson to conceive and pioneer many new sales methods, which resulted in the current size and success of the National Cash Register Company, a major corporation in the United States. In building this company, Patterson created the first manual of salesmanship, became the first to teach salesmanship with slides and other audiovisual devices, and pioneered the use of direct-mail marketing on a large scale.

Anyone who watches television is familiar with the American Express commercials. What viewers do not learn is that the American Express Travelers Cheque was the invention of American Express executive William Fargo. He conceived it because he had trouble getting cash in Europe, outside of capital cities, despite his letters of credit. Actually, Fargo turned the problem over to Marcellus Berry, who had earlier designed the American Express Money Order, and Berry came up with the idea of the two-signature check—one signature affixed by the bearer when the checks were issued, the other affixed when they were to be cashed, to validate the checks. Fargo saw a need and responded to it with another service, something of a variant from earlier services provided.

Flour milling a hundred years ago was a highly competitive business, and one small mill in Grand Forks, North Dakota, was on the verge of bankruptcy after the depression known as the Panic of 1893. Struggling to stay alive after that great panic, the partners were persuaded by their head miller, Tom Amidon, to permit him to package and offer for sale a "breakfast porridge" he had made from wheat and used in his own home. In fact, so broke were the owners of the mill that the first shipment of this new product was made in hand-assembled and hand-labeled boxes. The name assigned this new product was Cream of Wheat, and not too many years later the stock of Cream of Wheat Corporation was listed on the New York Stock Exchange.

There are, of course, hundreds of such stories: A large percentage of the fourteen million businesses in the United States owe their origins or their successes to such ingenuity in developing or adapting a product or service to satisfy a need hitherto unrecognized. Sometimes the need is not so much for a new product or new service as it is for a new marketing or distribution idea. For example, in the early to middle nineteenth century, there was no established system for small retail dealers to order stock, much of which came from Europe, in drugs and chemicals. Recognizing this, John McKesson and Charles Olcott established a partnership to serve as the middlemen-wholesalers of such merchandise. Later, this was to become the firm today known as

McKesson & Robbins, a major manufacturing and distributing firm handling drugs, liquor, and chemical products.

William Colgate opened his tiny shop at number 6 Dutch Street when he was just twenty-three years old. His first customer did not enter his shop until the first day was half gone, and young Colgate was all but biting his nails. When the elderly gentleman who was Colgate's first customer had selected and paid for a two-pound bar of soap, Colgate asked where the gentleman wanted the soap delivered. The customer was stunned: free delivery was unheard of in 1806. But Colgate insisted that his business was based on better service than was obtainable elsewhere, and that was how he founded the company that ultimately became known as the Colgate-Palmolive Company.

In 1909 Joseph French Johnson launched a business that has become something of an American institution. A Harvard graduate, Johnson became financial editor of the *Chicago Tribune* in 1886. He soon discovered, through his daily contacts with bankers and corporate executives, that few of them really understood finance or had had any formal training in the subject. However, no executive could or would even consider leaving work and attending a university course in the subject. Meanwhile, Johnson had left the newspaper to become professor of finance at the Wharton School of Finance and Commerce of the University of Pennsylvania in Philadelphia. He tried to set up an extension evening course, but the university found itself unable to support such a venture. At this point, Johnson found himself talking to a Chicago publisher who had the idea of publishing a set of books on the subject of finance and financial management. Out of these conversations came what is today the Alexander Hamilton Institute, which has trained over five hundred thousand executives by correspondence.

What is significant in each of these cases? Carl Wickman had the Hupmobile vehicle and no customers who needed it. What the available customers needed was transportation, and Wickman had the means to provide that transportation.

John Patterson originally became interested in cash registers because his store clerks were stealing him into bankruptcy. The cash register, crude as it was, rescued him by making it difficult for the clerks to steal. But when he bought a cash register manufacturing business, he found that other businessmen were not as receptive as he was and had to be sold hard. Of necessity, Patterson pioneered more effective sales training and sales methods.

American Express Travelers Cheques were born out of a perceived need of customers for a means to carry money over long distances, while still enjoying some degree of safety against losing the money or having it stolen. It was a classic case of finding a need and filling it.

Cream of Wheat was born out of a desperate necessity. In a sense, this was a case of creating a need. When a new product proves acceptable, a new need has been created.

In these and other cases cited here, *success was achieved by making changes,* by adapting to circumstances and needs. These entrepreneurs created new products, new services, new marketing systems, new appeals —sometimes driven by necessity, sometimes shrewdly exploiting a perceived opportunity, sometimes exercising vision denied others, and sometimes recognizing a need to advance, to step another rung up the ladder of progress, to acknowledge and respond to generally changing conditions and situations.

The latter situation is where a great many of us fail. If customers resist change and new ideas, so do the entrepreneurs who make offers to customers. It's rather widely acknowledged that anyone selling precisely what he or she sold five years ago is risking failure through obsolescence, and anyone attempting to sell the products and services of ten years ago is probably already dead, in a business sense, whether the condition is recognized or not. Yet, what we might call the buggy-whip-and-horseshoe syndrome is still very much in evidence, and is largely responsible for a great many business failures.

MARKETING IS NOT A ONE-TIME FUNCTION

The great error is this: Too often the entrepreneur conceives of marketing as done once, at the onset of the business, and never needed again. Many entrepreneurs develop successful marketing strategies, build successful programs based on those strategies, and then retire on the job, with the expectation that their organizations need merely to follow the master plan forevermore. If the strategies are successful enough, the company may go on for a number of years on that basis. But no one can keep the same advantage forever: It is necessary for even the most clever innovator to develop new and fresh innovations in order to *stay* ahead of competitors. You may be sure that if you are highly successful, you will have imitators.

Marketing must be a *continuous* function because you cannot keep the same advantage forever. Your long-term success depends on not a single strategy, but upon your ability to develop new ideas and to perceive, recognize, and understand the changes taking place. For example, if Robert Hall had seen some of the new style trends arriving, such as the craze for jeans, and responded to them, they would probably still be in operation today. In the end, it's a matter of needs and wants. Needs and wants change. Not radically—most people resist radical change—but gradually; most of us welcome gradual change, and in the long view, most change can be seen to have been gradual, at least in the sense that change is an outgrowth of what currently exists. Yet, despite the fact that the change must be gradual so that people do not find themselves forced to relinquish their grip on the familiar and secure, change is inevitable.

Some entrepreneurs have recognized that people are reluctant to yield their grip on the familiar and secure, and have turned this fact to their own advantage in what we might call the nostalgia business. Styles and artifacts of the twenties, thirties, and forties—and more recently, of the fifties—are in such demand that some alert people are even manufacturing items in those styles and succeeding in the marketplace with them. The demand is so strong that items only fifty or sixty years old are regarded as antiques and command high prices.

The market changes constantly too, sometimes for totally unpredictable reasons. The publicity given to President Reagan's taste for jelly beans has created a huge surge in the jelly-bean business, especially for the brand he prefers. Publicity is responsible for many successes, although they are often short-lived successes—as with the Hula Hoop and the Pet Rock. Changes of this type are extremely difficult to plan for and react to because they are unpredictable, both as to their incidence at all and as to their endurance. Many entrepreneurs lost money on the hoop toy, for example, because the demand was sudden, sharp, and short-lived—so short-lived that the demand had dropped almost to zero by the time these entrepreneurs had their products ready for market.

MARKETING METHODS CAN CHANGE, TOO

The changes that take place in the market are not necessarily a reflection of changing tastes or changing desires on the part of buyers. Sometimes the changes are the result of a marketer's imagination, and reflect a change in the way something is marketed. One such change was the book club, the brainchild of Maxwell Sackheim, acknowledged dean of mail-order copywriters. It didn't change the way books were sold, to be sure, but it added a new dimension to bookselling and introduced a method that did, in fact, sell a great many books, and has been widely imitated. There are a great many book clubs today, and one mark of success for an author is to have his or her book chosen by a book club as one of its selections.

The book club is representative of a specific marketing philosophy which champions an aggressive approach—active marketing, as contrasted with passive marketing.

ACTIVE VERSUS PASSIVE MARKETING METHODS

Most typical of passive marketing methods is the retail establishment. In the traditional retail marketing systems, the manufacturer markets or "distributes" the line through a network of wholesalers and retailers. The latter merchants display the merchandise in their establishments, where they must wait for customers to enter and decide to buy whatever strikes their fancy or satisfies their wants.

Some merchants are almost totally passive, making little or no special effort to bring traffic into their stores or to sell anything to their customers, preferring to wait until the customer decides. Other merchants are not content to wait for the customer to decide to enter the store or to decide what to buy; the merchant decides to do something *active* to induce customers into the place of business, and takes active steps to sell merchandise.

One well-established method for doing this is advertising, with the advertising messages offering arguments and reasons which, it is hoped, will persuade the customers to come in and order things. And there are merchants who content themselves with this degree of active marketing, but who do little else to provoke sales.

As a next step up the ladder of marketing and sales aggressiveness, there are merchants who are themselves good salespeople—aggressive and persuasive, registering a good degree of success in inducing customers to buy various items that the merchant decides to push. As a help in pushing certain items, the merchant will often feature the item in advertising, set up special displays in the store, and perhaps make special offers—sale prices, for example. Rebates, which are currently favored, were invented as a marketing device by the automobile manufacturers a few years ago, when automobile sales started to slump. For some reasons—psychological ones, that is—customers found the idea of getting a cash rebate more attractive than getting the same amount simply discounted from the original price. Presumably because customers are more sophisticated than they were a few years ago, they regard sale prices and discounts with a great deal of suspicion, but find the idea of a cash rebate far more believable. In any case, it has been a successful marketing ploy, and has been adopted rather widely by manufacturers of small appliances.

In-store demonstrations have been successful in marketing new items for which customers had to be "educated," either because the product was radically new and different or because it was significantly higher in price than competing items of the same general type. Nevertheless, such marketing and sales methods still are inherently passive in nature because they rely on customers visiting the retail establishment, and are thus essentially reactive. That is, the merchant must try to induce the customer to come to him or her to be sold. For the most part, customers come to the retail store to look things over before making final decisions about buying anything.

At the other end of the spectrum are marketing and sales methods that do not wait for customers to come to the retail establishment. Instead, they go to the customer in what is usually known as direct marketing or direct-response marketing. This type of marketing pursues the customer in a variety of ways: knock-on-the-door calls at customers' homes, mail solicitations, street-corner solicitations (e.g., sample distributions), direct-response advertising (e.g., magazine advertisements with order forms), and telephone solicitations.

This marketing philosophy says, "Let's not wait for the customer to call on us. Let's call on the customer." Many vacuum cleaners are sold this way, as are most encyclopedias. Fuller Brush, Avon, and many other companies sell this way exclusively, through door-to-door canvassing, and a great many companies sell through the mails.

There are also combinations of methods in which companies appoint dealers throughout the country, who sell independently by whatever methods they choose—usually as salespeople calling on prospects—with the orders filled by mail or other mode of shipment.

PROS AND CONS
OF THE TWO APPROACHES

There are many things to be said about each method. The passive methods offer certain advantages as well as disadvantages in marketing merchandise, as compared with more aggressive marketing systems: A retail establishment that waits for customers to enter can usually market the merchandise at a much lower selling cost. The retailer operating a store has relatively inexpensive clerical sales help, whereas the alternative method depends on salespeople-dealers who get as much as 40 percent of the selling price as their commission or profit. The typical retail establishment also has a better opportunity to make multiple sales to each customer, whereas direct-response marketing is often based on selling a single item.

On the other hand, whereas the retail merchant often can do nothing effective about a slow period when sales are sparse, direct-response marketers can compensate with added aggressiveness. The direct-response marketer who uses commission salespeople or dealers is not paying out salaries that represent complete losses during slow periods, as is the retail merchant operating a fixed establishment.

There is also the matter of personal preference, especially when the enterprise is young and the entrepreneur is doing all or nearly all things personally: Some individuals shrink from "cold" selling, while others approach it with great enthusiasm, and this has no doubt been a factor in establishing marketing philosophies for many of today's companies.

Perhaps the most influential factor of all has been the nature of the marketing problem itself. Some situations simply lend themselves better to one or the other marketing systems. In fact, some things would be most difficult to market at all if another system than the one actually in use were to be employed. For example, there are some products that people rarely buy unless some salesperson sells these products to them. Vacuum cleaners are one such case because door-to-door canvassing has been the traditional way of selling vacuum cleaners for many years, and it is nearly impossible to determine whether they can be sold effectively in any other manner. It has now become an article of faith. Some sales are made in the store, but these represent only a tiny portion of the total sales volume of vacuum cleaners.

However, there is an interesting facet to the sales that are made in retail stores. Except for a relative few sales made in department stores, vacuum cleaner sales are almost invariably made in *service* establishments, if not sold in door-to-door marketing. That is, dealers who repair vacuum cleaners are able to make a significant number of sales simply because they are in an ideal position to do so. They know the current condition of the customer's vacuum cleaner and what it will take to repair it, and they can compare the performance of the old vacuum cleaner, even when repaired, with the performance of a new vacuum cleaner which has many design improvements. Being the repair station confers many marketing advantages on the dealer, providing marketing or sales leverage.

Other items that are traditionally sold through direct-response methods—most often through door-to-door sales—are sewing machines, encyclopedias, magazine subscriptions, and home-improvement services. The latter are not usually sold on cold canvasses, but rather by direct-response, in-the-home sales presentations. Most often, these result from appointments set up by telephone, as the result of leads generated by advertising. This is something of a variant, and merits some explanation, for it is typical of another method of marketing which requires intensive selling effort, or which some people refer to as high-pressure selling. It involves using advertising to develop sales leads, and then following up the leads to close as many sales as possible. This saves time otherwise spent knocking on doors to find likely prospects.

THE CHOICES AVAILABLE

Aside from the basic classification of passive versus active marketing, there are numerous variants and hybrids. Passive marketing means that you wait for customers to come to you, to your place of business, although you may take measures to persuade them to come to you. On the other hand, active marketing refers to going to the customer—house-to-house canvassing, telephone solicitation, direct-mail marketing, and other methods by which you pursue the customer at home, in the office, on the streets, or elsewhere, other than in your own place of business.

Methods for bringing customers to your place of business include advertising special sales, premiums, giveaways, contests, and other promotions which persuade customers to make it a point to come to your establishment.

Calling on the customers at their homes or offices may be done by the "cold call" method, or it may be done by appointments set up as a result of using advertising or other methods to create sales leads.

To some extent, the choice may be arbitrary—it may be that method with which you are most comfortable. Some types of marketing and selling, particularly cold-call canvassing, are commonly associated with high-pressure tactics because most customers almost instinctively shrink from a sales contact they have not initiated. They assume, usually, that they are going to be high-pressured and become defensive immediately. For many merchants, this is an unpleasant selling environment and is to be avoided.

At the same time, this choice is not entirely arbitrary: The item offered for sale, as well as other circumstances, often dictate the marketing method. If you plan to sell home-improvement services, sitting in a retail store waiting for business is likely to result in cobwebs more than in anything else. Home improvement is not, and probably cannot be, sold this way. Such work involves a major financial commitment by the customer; and you must sell to both spouses, spending many hours at the sales effort before you get a signed contract.

Selling an item of this nature entails several distinct phases of marketing effort:

1. Developing leads—finding prospects for what you offer.
2. Setting up appointments where you can discuss the prospects' needs with them, vis-à-vis what you have to offer.
3. Preparing estimates and making the extended sales effort.

Each of these, especially the first phase, involves a great deal of effort. Once you are past the first phase, you are into the sales phase. For now, the important thing is to get good sales leads—*qualified* sales leads. And that is definitely a marketing function. It is, for the home-improvement business, the equivalent of getting customers into a retail store where you sell consumer commodities. In both cases, you are seeking prospects, whom you hope to turn into customers.

On the other hand, suppose you operate an automobile dealership. Here you are selling a big-tag item, and in most cases the customer will not buy without the spouse's approval. Here, too, you need prospects to work on, but you must get them to visit you, for you have to show them the car. And there is one other major difference between marketing home improvements and automobiles: You sell the same automobiles your competitors sell. Customers can call on other dealers who handle the same line and do comparison shopping, whereas the buyer of home improvements ordinarily buys a custom product and service and can't make direct comparisons. That changes the marketing problem considerably.

When you begin to analyze these factors and influences, you discover that you do not have as many options as you might at first have thought you had. These factors tend to dictate the marketing problem and therefore the marketing approaches available to you. The difference often comes down to this: To sell home improvement effectively, you must gain and keep the customer's confidence. Aside from the fact that there have been many home-improvement rip-offs and that therefore home-improvement firms tend to be automatically suspect simply because the customer can't go out and comparison shop readily, the customer realizes that he or she must depend on the dealer. Therefore, a major marketing problem is to inspire the customer's confidence, to convince the customer that you are honest, trustworthy, ethical, and so forth. In the automobile business, most dealers try to persuade customers that they can offer a lower price than can any other dealer. They reason, with some justification, that they've few weapons to combat competition because the cars are standard models, available freely, and easily susceptible to comparison shopping. This all but compels the automobile dealer to be something of a huckster, to employ high-pressure tactics, to stretch the truth pretty badly, to make promises he has no intention of keeping, and to otherwise use every means, fair or foul, to close sales.

However, very much the same condition applies in selling consumer commodities. The consumer tends to become brand conscious of a great many items because of heavy advertising and because, as in the case of automobiles, it is quite easy for the customer to comparison shop. It's quite easy to check the A & P's prices against Safeway's prices for many nationally known brands of different commodities. On the other hand, it's relatively difficult to do this with furniture and clothing—

although there are some nationally known brands, the public is not brand conscious and the goods are not amenable to comparison shopping on any but the most general basis.

This condition, then, dictates marketing strategy—at least it dictates whether you are going to have to cope successfully with comparison shopping, which means shopping for price.

Actually, this is a matter of determining the very nature of the market in general—the common condition you must accommodate your marketing to, along with your competitors. But there are other market conditions, conditions peculiar to you, and which you do *not* share with your competitors. These conditions are imposed by store location, by the type of customers you have to work with, and by any special problems or conditions. They may not always be problems; they may be peculiar advantages you have, and which you should exploit. For example, if you have better access to merchandise at bargain prices, you have an advantage, and it should be taken into account in your planning. There is also serendipity—a lucky discovery that you can take advantage of. Here is one such case: Ted opened an appliance store in the early days of TV, as did many others who believed they could make money retailing TV receivers. Ted's problem was that he had little capital, and couldn't put in much of a stock. He discovered that a hardware store down the street was stuck with a large stock of coffee makers they couldn't sell fast enough to justify the space they took up. They wanted to unload them en masse at two dollars each. Ted offered them one dollar each and to his surprise they accepted his offer, and Ted took delivery of six hundred coffee makers. He offered them to his own customers, with advertising and signs in his store window, at $6.95. It didn't take long for Ted to sell these out completely at a substantial profit. Shortly thereafter, Ted quietly liquidated his TV business and went seeking more wholesale bargains in merchandise, a business he has remained in and been successful with for many years.

To some extent you may be able to control the types of customers with whom you do business. Especially in the retail trade, a merchant can decide whether he will go after bargain-basement kinds of customers or the carriage trade. It's quite difficult to do both, unless you are so large that you can quite literally have a bargain basement or an outlet store in addition to your main emporium. At least in the beginning, when you are small and trying to get established, it is far better to make a decision to pursue one kind of customer or the other. If you have all kinds of hand-painted specials scrawled on your windows or on tacked-up poster boards, you will not attract most people with wealth and discriminating tastes. And if you have a carpeted establishment, with acoustic-tile ceiling, soft music playing in a generally hushed atmosphere, and prices to suit such surroundings, you are not likely to attract many blue-collar workers and their families.

However, there are some factors that may dictate what kind of trade you will have. One of these factors is location, if yours is the kind of business that requires the customers to visit you. Another is the nature of what you offer for sale. If you deal in inexpensive jewelry and novelties, you have already selected your trade: The carriage trade does not ordinarily buy *in*expensive jewelry.

Sometimes markets spring up overnight (and sometimes vanish almost as quickly). The Kennedy administration caused a bull market in rocking chairs for a while, and the Reagan presidency has created a demand for a certain brand of jelly beans that has major department stores begging for supplies. Those who sense the trend quickly enough and move swiftly often realize enormous benefits in a short time. Conversely, those who fail to recognize that a market has faded or is fading rapidly are in an excellent position to lose heavily.

OTHER IMPORTANT ELEMENTS TO ANALYZE

You must recognize that you are dealing with people, as well as with a great many other factors, some of which you have control over and some of which you have little or no control over. You selected what you thought was a suitable location; you have fixtures, furnishings, inventory, advertising, and other assets in whatever quality and quantity you can afford. You have tried to decide what the marketing requirements are to make a success of the enterprise. In the end it all comes down to *motivating prospects* so that they become customers. It all comes down to *people,* the people you plan to convert into customers: into making accurate evaluations of what will make your prospects buy and thus become *your* customers.

CUSTOMER MOTIVATIONS

We know that in general customers buy goods and services for what those goods and services will do for them—make them attractive, lend prestige, provide security, make them feel good, etc.—all emotional appeals. So, a first order of business in the marketing analysis is to decide what the inherent benefits are in the goods or services we offer.

Let's take that home-improvement business as one case. Why should anyone go into debt to remodel, renovate, modernize the home in which they are living? What are the benefits that are *emotionally* appealing?

Remember that in this case, as in many others, we have two selling jobs to do:

1. We must first convince the prospect that he or she should renovate the house.
2. We must convince the prospect that he or she should buy from *us*.

Our marketing strategy must therefore address two major motivational themes: the benefits of home remodeling and the benefits of doing business with yours truly.

Developing the motivational strategy is primarily a matter of asking yourself the right questions. For example, if I were Mr. and Mrs. Prospect, what would turn me on about the idea of remodeling my house? The answers I came up with and which of those I decided were most powerful should determine the basis for the marketing attack. The next question would be this: How can I best reach my prospects with the message—the promise that remodeling their old home is going to do so much for them?

REACHING PROSPECTS

Of course, before we can study methods for reaching our prospects, we have to be sure we know who our prospects are—not *what* they are (rich, poor; white-collar, blue-collar; young, old; etc.): We need to know where they live and work, where they vacation, where they play, what they read, and all the other factors that will help us determine how to get our message *to* the specific group of prospects.

Depending on how we are organized to do business, we may want to seek business all over town, all over the county, all over the state, or perhaps only in our part of town. Making that determination helps us fix our target: We now know both who and what our prospects are—what they have in common, what their typical financial situation is, what kinds of homes they typically own.

If most of the prospects we have identified live in older homes, virtually all of our work will probably be renovation and remodeling. But, if some significant percentage live in modern suburban homes not likely to be in need of remodeling or modernization, we may wish to offer services to provide add-ons and to expand the living space.

We already know that in order to sell home-improvement remodeling, the best marketing methodology is to first develop sales leads by advertising that motivates prospects to call or write so that we can make appointments to talk to them. The reasonable presumption is that anyone who calls or writes in response to our advertising or promotion is at least mildly interested in the prospect of remodeling or adding on to his or her home.

Straight advertising, explaining what you offer and why the prospect ought to consider it, will bring in some inquiries. In all probability, that response is going to be far less than you need. Usually it takes something more than straight advertising to do the job. Another alternative is the home show, or other shows and exhibits in which you may participate, with a demonstration booth, sales literature, and sales representatives. Because there are almost always numerous competitors there, you need something more than an exhibit booth. Most exhibitors offer prizes, give away novelty items, and do other things to (1) attract visitors to pick up their literature and listen to sales presentations and (2) register their names, addresses, and telephone numbers, often as part of entering the prize contest. Of course, each visitor so registering is a specific prospect who will be called to see if an appointment can be made. If the sales representative at the booth had an opportunity to draw the visitor into conversation, the exhibitor may have some special notes on that prospect's special concerns and interests! Another inducement sometimes used is to offer prospects a free energy audit in their homes, which automatically sets up an appointment and gives the sales representative an opportunity to look around the home for readily apparent needs.

However, in any advertising or sales promotion, the first consideration is to reach the prospects you want to reach. It would be little use, for example, to advertise in *Popular Mechanics* if you were intent on reaching nuclear engineers, for it is doubtful that many nuclear engineers read that publication. More to the point, if you are trying to reach the typical male homeowners of your town, probably the sports pages of your daily newspaper would be a good way. Or you may be able to reach prospects by telephone solicitation. To do this, you would hire people—often housewives who can't leave their homes to take a regular nine-to-five job, but who would do telephone soliciting a few hours a day. They would try to set up appointments, and would be paid some fee for each appointment they succeeded in setting up. Of course, you would have to provide them with the basic sales message, but you might find this a most efficient way to develop sales leads.

This is not a matter to be left entirely up in the air until the time comes. It's something to be considered before making the entrepreneurial commitment, for this reason: You must be reasonably certain that you can reach those prospects you have targeted. Otherwise, all your other efforts are in vain.

Let us suppose, for example, that you have somehow come up with a service or product that every surgeon in the country is almost sure to want, once it becomes known. But, after you have gone to great trouble and expense to get yourself ready to do business, you suddenly discover that you have no way to reach these prospects except by an exorbitantly expensive and wasteful program. Unless you can afford to waste most of your advertising and promotional dollars, and unless the profit margin in your enterprise is great enough to absorb such costly waste, your enterprise is stillborn. Of course, you can always reach prospects wastefully, as you will learn in the chapter on advertising, by such wide broadcasting that it takes in virtually everyone, although only one tenth of 1 percent is of value to you. But reaching prospects means reaching them on some reasonably efficient basis. That's a must. Otherwise the marketing cost will itself sink the enterprise.

"GO" AND "NO GO" FACTORS

In analyzing the market—and what you must do to succeed in that market with your offer—you should have recognized that some of the data you are collecting is of the must-know variety, other data is in the very-helpful class, and the remaining information is useful but not essential. That is, you absolutely must know who and what your prospective customers are, how to reach them and make your offer, and what they want. Also, it would be most helpful to know something of what your competitors are doing and how they are marketing. Ultimately, you'll learn this whether you make a special effort or not, as a result of doing business every day. However, there are a few factors that are so critically important as to be "go" or "no go" indicators.

One of these is the potential benefit of your product or service to the customer. Difficult as this is to identify accurately, it is probably the single most important factor in your eventual success or failure. It explains why the Nehru jacket, the Edsel, and other ventures were such dismal—and costly—failures: The prospects simply did not perceive adequate benefits resulting from the purchase. And there are many such failures. For the most part, we don't hear much about them, especially if they never really got off the ground. But most of them nevertheless represent classic marketing failures—the entrepreneurs in most cases failed to do their marketing homework.

Another critically important factor that can spell the difference between dismal failure and a fighting chance to succeed is a clear plan for reaching the selected prospects at acceptable cost. Unless you can do this, you might just as well be offering something for which there are no prospects, or not enough of them to constitute a fair market. This is a two-pronged factor: You must be sure that there *is* a market, in the sense that there are *enough* prospects who are likely to want what you are offering; but you must also be sure that you have a reliable means for reaching these prospects in sufficient numbers to constitute a large enough market. However, don't make the mistake of reasoning that because you need to make two thousand sales per year to have a viable business, and there are five thousand identifiable prospects, you have an adequate market. It is most unlikely that you will capture 40 percent of any given market, whether you are introducing something brand new or are selling against established competition. You are more likely to capture 2 or 3 percent of the market, and will be doing very well if you ultimately capture 10 percent of the market. If you need two thousand sales per year, you had better be able to identify the potential for at least fifty times that number of sales annually.

A first go/no-go factor, then, is: *Will the prospects accept my offer as I have presented it?* Since prospects buy or do not buy primarily according to whether they perceive a desirable enough result occurring, how you present the offer may make the difference between acceptance and rejection. Perhaps nothing would have saved the Nehru jacket or the Edsel. On the other hand, perhaps some smart promotion would have made the Nehru jacket a success. George Jessel and Sammy Davis, Jr., were probably the only prominent entertainers to wear it in public, but what might have happened if the manufacturer had given complimentary jackets to a number of other entertainers? Would not the millions of prospects have succumbed to the suggestion of an "in" style if Johnny Carson and a few other popular people in the public eye had appeared wearing the jacket?

Many theories have been advanced as to why the Edsel failed, but it seems almost certain that bad timing was one factor—it was a bad year generally for the automobile industry—plus some styling that made the new car the butt of many jokes. Perhaps nothing was really done that badly by the Ford Motor Company, but circumstances conspired to create a $250 million disaster. There is no doubt that some ventures fail, despite the backers doing everything they could conceivably have done, and getting all the right signals suggesting a go-ahead and eventual success. Marketing is never an absolute science, at best. However, by far the majority of marketing failures—and almost all business failures can be shown to be marketing failures—result from failure to do all that can be done. The failure could also be caused by the playing of hunches by the principals in the venture, who tend too often to rely on their instincts—or what they believe are instincts, but which are often merely flashes of wishful thinking. Often the individual has conceived some new idea that involves his or her prestige, and he or she has difficulty in abandoning the great plan even when there is evidence that it won't work. Many companies devote great resources to pushing some product that customers firmly resist buying: The executive whose brainchild the product is will not give up trying to be right, no matter what it costs! This is the condition that has led to the wry observation so often heard that "Ten percent of our sales effort accounts for ninety percent of our sales, and ninety percent of our sales effort accounts for the other ten percent of our sales."

WHEN IS THE MARKET ANALYSIS COMPLETE?

Market analysis is never complete because markets must be constantly analyzed: They change almost continually. Rarely does the initial market analysis produce all the verifiable data desired. For example, one of the critical factors is identifying the result most customers will want to get from accepting your offer. How can you determine what this is? You can send people out to conduct surveys and interview typical prospects. The data you get back from this activity will be helpful, but not conclusive, for there are problems with these kinds of investigations, such as the "Hawthorne effect." This was so named because it was observed when evaluating results of a test conducted in an industrial plant in Hawthorne, California. Briefly, the effect observed was the very fact that what was being conducted was a test, which affected the results so that they did not accurately reflect what would probably happen in the equivalent operational situation. (In the world of physics, an analogous principle is known as the uncertainty principle or the Heisenberg effect.)

Therefore, the marketing plan—which should be fashioned after the market analysis is completed—should include plans for conducting tests; later, after the tests have been conducted, the results should be carefully considered before the final decision is made to proceed. In short, the conclusions drawn as a result of the market analysis ought to be confirmed by the tests before the entrepreneur makes the final decision to commit money and effort. The tests (to be described and discussed in the next two chapters) come much closer to simulating the actual conditions under which the product or service will be marketed, and the results are usually much more dependable than those resulting from simple surveys and interviews. Negative results do not mean the abandonment of the venture; negative results may mean only that there is a flaw in the marketing plan, which must be corrected. Ergo, the tests ought to be so designed as to *diagnose* the problem. It may have occurred to you that if the early surveys and interviews are not absolutely reliable indicators, why bother with them at all? Why not go straight to the tests?

To do that would be a greater mistake; it would result in testing an undeveloped idea. In the analysis, you should be getting some useful information from prospects about their preferences. That should affect such items as sizes offered, pricing, packaging, and what customers tell you they expect the product or service to do for them, as well as other factors, which you will later test specifically. Perhaps the people you talk to appear equally divided between their preferences for a small size, a large size, and a giant size. Does that mean that you should offer all three sizes? Tests will tell you, because you should then try all three sizes and see what happens. Don't be surprised if only one of the sizes sells well;

the phenomenon of people saying one thing, especially in a survey, and doing another is not at all unusual. That's one key reason for testing—to see if the people *do* what they say they will do.

SCOUTING THE COMPETITION

In some enterprises it's fairly easy to scout the competition: Collect and study their print ads, their TV commercials, their contests, their special sales promotions, their pricing, their various marketing and sales programs. If there are a large number of competitors, you will find soon enough that there are certain things common to the market—pricing and product sizes, for example, tend to fall into fairly close groupings—and certain things that are peculiar to each firm—for example, the basic benefit promised. One toothpaste firm promises "good checkups," while another concentrates on promising that their toothpaste includes both a dental cleanser and a breath sweetener. One appeals to parents with the implied promise that their children can reduce the need for dental work—cavities—by using their product; the other promises that users of their product won't offend spouses and lovers when kissing. Both have the same sizes available, and they are priced reasonably close to each other.

In other businesses it's not that easy to scout the competition, because some businesses do not do a great deal of media advertising. The only truly effective way to get the information you want about competition is from spying. One way to do that is to recruit the competitor's salespeople—or at least run advertisements to lure them in so that you can interview them and ask questions.

MARKET RESEARCH

There is a strong tendency on the part of those working primarily in the field of market research to focus their vision almost entirely on the mathematical side of market research—demographics, market share, and population density, etc. Important though this is, it neglects the qualitative side of market research, which is also important. Moreover, when making marketing decisions or *any* business decision based entirely on mathematical probabilities, bear in mind that these statistical probabilities work and are reliable only when the population is large enough. That is to say that if your market research reveals that 3 out of 10 housewives use a bleach, it does not follow that out of the 500 homes in your subdivision, 150 use bleach. That 3-out-of-10 figure is based on a much larger sample than 500, and is almost surely a figure arrived at in a *national* survey.

It has been noted that people being surveyed often say things they do not mean or, at least, their later actions do not match their words. However, sometimes people being surveyed are falsely accused of acting differently from their stated intentions. The fault may lie in the way questions are phrased or answers solicited. For example, if people are surveyed on their reaction to a new product, and they tend to agree that they would buy it, does this mean that they have already agreed that they would *switch brands,* or are they merely stating that they would *try* the new product? Ergo, don't ask if they will *buy*; ask if they will *try*.

Questioning people in a group produces different results than questioning them individually and privately. In a group, individuals will usually tend strongly to respond as others do, trying to conform. They are more likely to speak frankly when speaking privately. But group dynamics can be helpful when used properly. Getting a group to discuss a subject, such as the pros and cons of a new product or service, is different than asking for each attendee's individual opinion. The discussion is likely to produce highly useful information if the group is a reasonably typical cross-section of the prospects you wish to reach.

Market research can be divided into a large number of specific research efforts, each appropriately named. For example, in trying to find out what will best motivate a prospect to buy your product, you might be conducting *benefit* research, probing for what the customer wants the product to do. You might also be probing customer reaction to your product or to competitive products by conducting *problem* research, asking people what objections they have to the product or what problems they have encountered with its use.

People being interviewed often try to give the interviewer what they think is the "right" answer, rather than a completely frank answer. One way to overcome this problem is to conduct a most informal interview, with stimuli such as samples of the products, advertisements, and other related materials. This starts the interviewee talking more freely. Don't interrupt too often with questions; just encourage the free flow of talk along the "stream of consciousness" mode. Frequently you not only get insight into problems and customer objections, but into solutions, as well. In such situations, interviewees sometimes speak from their own subconscious, uttering opinions they didn't even know they held because they never thought about the matter before.

One thing to bear in mind: To a great extent, a major purpose in market research is to develop hypotheses or premises to test, to confirm or refute. Regard everything you learn, or think you learn, in research as something *more* to test. Regard the process as following the general lines of Figure 4.

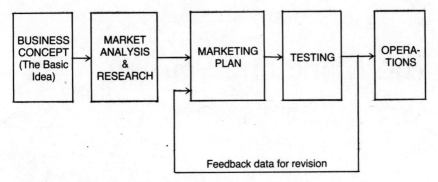

FIGURE 4. Major phases in marketing.

Note that the output of the tests consists of information that is used as feedback to revise the marketing plans—prospect profiles and demographic data, advertising copy, sales literature, and other vital elements of the marketing approaches.

7
The Marketing Plan

If marketing is to be intelligently directed, it must have distinct objectives.

WHY YOU NEED
A MARKETING PLAN

You started your venture with an idea, an idea to sell some product or service and an idea of how you would sell it. You had some reason to believe that you would succeed—not necessarily a good reason, but a reason. You may have thought that it was a can't-miss business or that you had a can't-miss idea—perhaps a new product or service, perhaps a new way of marketing, perhaps a better source of supply than others have. You may have had any of dozens of possible reasons for wishing to venture as you did.

If you did as you should have done, before you actually committed yourself firmly to the venture, you did some market research and analysis as a first step in checking out your ideas and seeing if they seem to be viable. You talked to people, conducted surveys and interviews, talked to potential competitors, gathered as much information as possible. So far, what you have learned appears to bear out your original idea that the business plan is reasonably sound, and you should have a fair chance of succeeding. You may have modified some of your original ideas a bit—perhaps there is more competition or tougher competition than you originally thought, but since they are all making a living at the business, there is no reason to believe that there is not room for one more. In any case, you haven't come up with anything to change your mind about undertaking the venture. So it is now time to begin serious planning, and the first order of business is the development of a marketing plan. This does not mean necessarily that the plan will be a two-hundred-page typed document, with charts and drawings, bound in a fancy plastic folder. For a small venture, the plan might be quite a modest set of notes in a notebook, handwritten and intended for only your own eyes. But it should be documented, for many reasons.

You need it as a road map. You can't expect your mind to retain all the details you have worked out. Moreover, you will want to amend it as you go along and gain new knowledge, and you'll need to record that information, for it will have cost you money and it will be important to the eventual success of your business. So take the trouble to record your plan in some manner, no matter how informally.

If you are going to do some testing—and it is highly desirable that you do so, to reduce the risks and increase the probability of success—regard that marketing plan as preliminary. After test results are in and are evaluated, you will almost surely want to make some changes in the marketing plan, for it is not very likely that all your estimates, guesses, and preliminary data are right on the nose.

Before you decide that you can do without the cost and lost time involved in testing and choose to go ahead without testing, consider this: Whether you conduct these tests or not, your marketing plan is going to change before long. Why? Because you will still learn, eventually, what is good and what is bad about your original plan, and you'll know eventually what works and what doesn't. The only difference is that without testing, it may take you a much longer time to learn this, and that will have cost you not only a great deal more money than the tests would have, but may have cost you your entire investment if the venture fails before you learn what you need to know to make it succeed.

Before long you will learn that testing is not necessarily either costly or wasteful. In fact, it is more likely to save you both time and money.

THE ELEMENTS OF THE MARKETING PLAN

Marketing, according to Dr. Philip Kotler of the graduate school of management at Northwestern University, includes analyzing, planning, and controlling those forces or factors that make the market or impact the prospective customer. I've no quarrel with that. In fact, it fits rather well here in defining what belongs logically in the marketing plan.

The main focus of the marketing plan is what a psychologist or sociologist might refer to as the "target population"—the people to whom you wish to present your offer and whom you hope to make your customers. If the chief purpose of a business is to create customers, as Peter Drucker has said, then people—prospective customers—are what the marketing plan is about, principally. The first element of the marketing plan is, then: ·

PROSPECTS
    Who they are
    What they are
    Where they are
    How to reach them
        Advertising
            Where, when, how much
        Other
            Trade shows/conventions/conferences/home shows/etc.
            Telephone solicitation
            Newsletters, advertising specialties, contests, sponsorship of bowling teams, etc.
        What to offer
        Benefits to promise
COMPETITION
    Who, rank in order
    Where
    How strong
    Main strengths, main weaknesses
    How they market
BASIC STRATEGY FOR MARKETING
    Active versus passive marketing
    Direct response
    Prospecting for leads
    Advertising approach
    Main promotional approach
    Secondary strategy
    Strategy for meeting competition
BUDGET
    Allocations for all marketing activities
FORECASTS
    Estimating results
CONTROLS
    Establish results required (cutoff points for advertising, other promotion)
TESTING
    What is to be tested?
        Definition of prospects (demographics)
        Main marketing strategy
        Customer motivation
        Advertising
        Other sales promotion
        Prices
        Sales tools
        Product or service (customer acceptance)

PROSPECTS

Identifying the prospects you plan to sell to is often referred to as *demographics*. That's a fancy name for vital statistics—who, what, where, and when. Demographics tells you where prospects live, what their average income is, what kind of work they do, what percentage own their own homes, and a wide variety of other such data, much of it useful. How do you get this data? Easy: Much of it is available free of charge or at very little cost from the U.S. Department of Commerce, Bureau of the Census. Write them and they will tell you just what they have available and how to get what you want. Bear in mind that this data just may not be helpful to you in your own case if you are engaged in a strictly local business and have quite a clear idea about your prospects and the relevant demographics.

In any case, you should write out some kind of description of your prospects, what their general interests are likely to be, and how you plan to reach them. If by advertising, where and how will you advertise? Newspaper? Billboards? Direct mail? Radio? TV? And, of course, for any of these you plan to use, you'll need some further details, which we'll be discussing later, when we talk about advertising. You'll want to note here, also, any special promotions, such as booths in conventions or trade shows, sponsorship of a bowling league or Little League ball club, publishing a newsletter (that is, a free newsletter for sales promotion, which has worked well for some businesses), telephone solicitations, or whatever methods you believe will be effective in reaching the prospects.

Bear in mind, in all of these and other areas of the marketing plan, that you are not making a permanent commitment to pursue every item you have projected in your marketing plan. You may wish to test several methods to find the most effective one, after which you will drop others. The decision is yours, of course, but the factors controlling the decision are most likely to be economic ones. Here is a sensible way to analyze this, assuming that you do have limits on available funds and can't do everything you'd like to try out.

1. List all the ways your competitors advertise and promote.
2. Rank in order the items on that list, with the most widely used marketing promotion method first, and the others in declining order.
3. Compare what you have with your own original ideas of what you planned to use. If the two lists differ sharply, you ought to give this some serious thought. It's reasonable to assume that your competitors have tried out all the other ways and found them wanting, and that they are using the methods that experience shows work best.

This is intended to reduce the risks and to keep you from reinventing the wheel—wasting a great deal of money to verify that your competitors are right in what they are doing. Still, as one New York advertising man puts it, "What works for P&G, doesn't work for you and me." And the reverse is also true: What does not work for a competitor may very well work for you. Therefore, it is probably an excellent idea, if you can afford it, to test the methods in most common use against the methods you propose to use, and see what works best—for *you*.

When you make these tests, there is one other factor to consider: the immediacy of the response to your advertising and promotional methods. There are some promotional methods that are highly effective *over a long period of time,* but do not produce *rapid results.* For example, putting an advertisement in the newspaper, with a coupon and perhaps some special gift for the first one hundred people who call or write, does produce immediate results, if at all, because of the nature of the advertising. Few people will clip such an advertisement and save it. On the other hand, sponsoring a bowling league and giving away jackets with your business name on the backs is likely to produce business sometime in the fairly distant future. This difference has to be taken into account in two respects.

1. If your situation is such that you must have early results to survive, stay away from those promotions and advertisements with only long-term benefits. You can't afford them.

2. If you think you can afford some long-term advertising and promotion of this sort, be sure to recognize this in your tests, and don't compare the order-getting power of bowling jackets with that of newspaper and radio advertising.

The benefits you are going to offer—the *motivators* you will provide to induce prospects to become interested and to buy—are not unrelated to the prospect characteristics. Let's consider, for example, the following profile of a typical prospect you might be pursuing for home-improvement contracts:

OCCUPATION:	Blue-collar
AGE:	20–45
RESIDENCE:	Ranges from row house to suburban, 3 BR
NEIGHBORHOOD:	Typical working class, middle economic scale
EDUCATION:	High school graduate
FAMILY:	2 children at home, in school
INCOME:	$25–30,000; likely that wife works, at least part-time

Experience might show that this profile of your *most likely* prospects is in error. Logic suggests this. For one thing, young marrieds in their early twenties are less likely to become customers for at least two reasons: (1)

Young marrieds are usually barely getting by economically, and (2) they have probably bought a house which will be adequate for them for ten years or more, and they are not likely to feel a need for change before then. Consequently, at least as far as the younger portion of this prospect population is concerned, they are not likely to be motivated by the promise of additional space, a game room to entertain their friends, etc., as the older portion of the population might be. However, this is only theory, based on what appears to be logical deduction. Experience —surveying and testing, as well as actual business experience—might well prove otherwise. Perhaps economic pressures have compelled the young marrieds to buy smaller homes than they would have wished to, and they feel forced to add a nursery or bedroom to the house as their young families grow.

A different logic applies to the older group of prospects. For many of them, the house has become more spacious because the children have grown, gone to work, and moved out, leaving them with more space than they need, and with less expense, as well. Many couples in this situation sell their homes, buy condominiums, or otherwise trade up. But today's real estate cost has broken the pattern: Many couples feel that they cannot handle the high costs of trading up, and they must make do with what they have. Therefore, their motivator may well be that it's far cheaper to modernize their present home and render it more appropriate to a couple without children at home by adding a recreation room, remodeling a bedroom to serve as a guest room, modernizing the kitchen into the model Mrs. Prospect always wanted, but could never afford before, and so on.

Again, these are theories; each must be tested. Almost any salesman will tell you that for all major expenditures, and especially for home improvement, it's important to get the wife's approval. If you fail to win her over and motivate her, you are most unlikely to make the sale. On the other hand, if you do turn her on to the idea of a new kitchen or a fancy guest room, Mr. Prospect is most likely to try to please her. A smart salesperson might play on guilt a bit—the argument that "now you can have that kitchen you always wanted" lays a bit of guilt on many husbands by suggesting that they were not quite as good providers as they might have been, and many marketers play on this emotion. (Read some insurance advertisements to verify this.)

Overall, in the home-improvement business you are more likely to make sales to the older marrieds for a variety of reasons, not excluding the fact that their homes are likely to be older, and therefore better candidates for improvement projects or modernizing.

In any case, you develop these arguments and motivators as you do the marketing plan—in stages or phases:

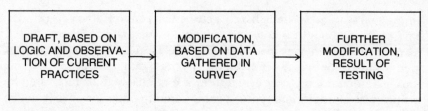

| DRAFT, BASED ON LOGIC AND OBSERVA-TION OF CURRENT PRACTICES | → | MODIFICATION, BASED ON DATA GATHERED IN SURVEY | → | FURTHER MODIFICATION, RESULT OF TESTING |

FIGURE 5. Refining the prospect profile.

COMPETITION

One common cause of failure in business ventures is underestimating the competition. The failures of such major corporations as General Electric and RCA to succeed in the computer field demonstrates that even the most successful of companies has to struggle to compete successfully when entering a new field. A much smaller company, Honeywell, has managed to remain successfully in the computer field. One major reason is that Honeywell markets most aggressively against the competition (mainly IBM) by maintaining extensive competitor files and a specific group of competitor specialists in its marketing group.

As in the case of all other marketing data, the scouting of the competition is not a one-time function: It must be carried on continually and kept up to date. When competitors shift gears, you must know it. And you must know *why*. In computers, for example, a newer company is marketing what they call the Apple computer. They've been quite successful because they are "where the competition ain't," manufacturing and marketing small computers for small businesses, with an eye peeled for the potential market for computers in private homes. If Apple is to stay healthy and continue to succeed against IBM, Control Data, Honeywell, and Burroughs, they will have to stay alert and try to keep a step ahead or, at least, in step with the competition.

In scouting the competition, you need to know exactly how they do their marketing, what their sales arguments are, precisely what goods and services they offer, what their prices are, what and where their successes are, and where their failures are. If a competitor is weak in service, he's a failure in the service area. Or if he is weak in service only in some specific geographic area, you want to know that, too. Just as the young men who founded the Apple company saw a gap not properly exploited by the existing companies and took advantage of that, so you may well be able to exploit some weakness or failure on the part of your own competitors to gain the advantage.

Answering such questions about your competitors as, How strong are they? How big are they? and How much business do they do? cannot

102

be done overall and be very helpful, for that reason. Rarely is any company equally strong everywhere. And "everywhere" means more than geographic location. It encompasses the whole spectrum of prod--ucts and services the competitor offers, over the whole spectrum of sales and marketing activities, and across the whole spectrum of customer relations and administrative functions.

For example, I discontinued doing business with one supplier of copying equipment because of poor service. Others I knew assured me that they got good service from this company, but I soon learned that the reason they received good service was that they were in a geographic area with a large population of this company's machines. Therefore, the company's service technicians were in the area constantly and able to provide fast service. That's a situation a competitor can exploit; but first he must know that the situation exists.

There are companies who are quite proficient in what they do, technically, but who are deficient in customer relations—again, a situation to be exploited. Once I changed printers, although the shop I dealt with gave me good printing service, because their bills were constantly in error, and they were surly about correcting them. I objected to the need to spend time double-checking every statement I got, but I objected even more to being verbally abused when I insisted that they review the work orders and correct their statements.

Wherever you can find a competitor weakness, you have an opening to consider ways to exploit the situation. You can almost always find some weakness that you can exploit rather than meet competitors head-on where they have all the advantages.

You may be selling directly or indirectly against the competition. The difference? In some lines—such as computers, automobiles, major appliances—and in many other cases where the expenditure is a significant one, the customer is busy gathering quotations from several sources. You may very well be bidding directly against all of your competitors, and the decisive factor may be price, but it may also be something else, such as service and guarantees. In any case, in such lines, most of your sales require that your bid be compared directly with those of competitors.

In other lines, such as in typical retail stores, the competition is indirect. Customers do not necessarily make a direct comparison of your prices and quality with those of your competitors, but develop a general preference for certain establishments they deal with.

In both cases it is necessary to know as much as possible about your competition, although the influences are far more subtle in the second case. Frequently, in a venture where the proprietor meets the customers face to face, the success of the venture is due primarily to the proprietor's personality or sales ability. A case in point is that of a Long Island company named Semi-Specialists of America, Inc. The company was founded by William Kelly, still chief executive officer of the company and still its star salesman among the twenty-four salespeople employed there. In the beginning, Kelly was the sole salesman for the company, as well as its chief executive. Kelly was always a top salesman, even when he worked for other people, and he attributes his success as a salesman to his willingness to go out of his way to find a scarce item for a customer, even when the order is so small that the time spent finding the item results in a loss, rather than a profit. But this kind of service creates the relationship and sets the tone that leads to larger orders and new accounts.

A basic failure in many marketing campaigns is the unwillingness or inability to analyze competitors' marketing methods with true objectivity, in the search for weaknesses. Take the automobile-retailing business as an example. One weakness in how most automobile dealers market is that they persuade customers to come to their showrooms. Thus, the prospect, not the dealer, has the initiative. What would happen if the situation were reversed—if the dealer called on the prospects?

One Washington, D.C.-area salesman did just that: He sells a high-priced, luxury car, and he does not wait for prospects to come to the showroom. Instead, he seeks out all the most successful business people in the area and calls on them, driving a fully equipped model of the car he wishes to sell. He insists that the prospect use the car for a day or two—no obligation, of course. He is reported to be setting sales records, despite the automobile-retailing problems of today.

BASIC STRATEGY FOR MARKETING

Your marketing plan will have to be based on a general marketing strategy, either active or passive. The pros and cons of each have already been discussed in some detail and do not need repeating here. But in your marketing plan, you must provide for the articulation of your basic strategy. That means *specifics* of how you propose to advertise, develop sales leads, participate in trade shows, and/or whatever other marketing approaches you choose. If advertising, for example, where and how—in what media; asking for what (orders? inquiries?)? Are you trying to develop sales leads or produce orders directly from the advertising? Will you use distributors or are you a distributor? Will you use direct-response methods? Or will you use inquiry advertising to build a mailing list, and then go to direct mail? Will you market through demonstrations and other point-of-sales methods in department stores, malls, shows, and other such places?

You have these and many other possible methods as alternatives, but you must make a choice and then focus your marketing strength by choosing one basic strategy and concentrating on it. Don't dissipate your marketing by trying all the methods at once; that's an almost sure way to fail.

It is usually wise to opt for a main strategy and earmark an alternative or secondary strategy as a fallback position, should the main strategy fail to produce the results you want.

BUDGET AND FORECASTS

Unless you've a bottomless pocket and money is of no concern, you need to have a budget established. You have to decide in advance just how much money you can afford to put into the marketing aspect of the venture, and how much should be allocated for advertising, printing, postage, and whatever other expenses you will have.

Marketing is a basic cost which must be recovered, along with all other costs, before your venture can show a profit. Presumably, you know what your other costs are—the fixed expenses for your establishment. You have also established a selling price which ordinarily must be competitive. Somewhere, in that difference between what you can charge and your costs, you must be able to accommodate your marketing costs and still show a profit. You can then set a sales target—the number of sales you must make to recover all costs and show a profit. Obviously, unless you know what results are necessary to constitute a successful venture, you won't know whether to proceed or not. That's why you need to have all the requirements worked out in advance, and that's why you must test your plans, unless you are willing to risk a large disaster.

TESTING

The most basic objective of testing is to determine whether your marketing plan is a good one or not. If the venture shows a substantial profit, well and good. You may wish to proceed on the basis tested without further delay. However, if it is marginal—if it shows the barest of profits or only breaks even or if it turns up a loss—you will have to either abandon the venture entirely or modify it considerably.

If the test is a simple "go/no go" test, showing only that the plan works or doesn't work, you won't know what to fix or how to fix it, and you'll have the distasteful prospect of making arbitrary changes and testing again, a highly inefficient way of developing your final marketing plans. To avoid this, it is necessary to design your tests to be diagnostic, so that if things do not go as well as you hoped, you'll understand and you'll know what to do about it.

Tests are only properly diagnostic if you plan them to be so. You must design the diagnostic indicators into the plan so that you can analyze the results. When Joe Sugarman launched his JS&A Group with his initial mail-order venture, selling the then-new pocket calculator, he lost half his investment. When he analyzed the results of his first mailing, he discovered that two of his mailing lists had actually shown a profit; it was the others that had done so poorly they dragged the entire venture down to a staggering loss. Putting the knowledge gained in the first mailing to work in a follow-up campaign, Sugarman more than recovered his early losses and started on the road to an eventual outstanding success as a multimillion-dollar company. Had he not been able to diagnose what went wrong, he might well have abandoned the venture entirely. His campaign was carried out by direct mail, and one of the prime items to be tested was the set of mailing lists. Since he was selling pocket calculators, Sugarman reasoned quite logically that accountants and engineers ought to be his most enthusiastic buyers. He was wrong. Presidents of companies doing one million dollars or more of business annually proved to be the best buyers, and it was the list of the latter that provided profitable mailings. That's a most basic lesson: What you and I think is logical "ain't necessarily so." You can only be sure by testing and then analyzing the tests.

However, there are other things you might want to test, depending on what your marketing approaches are and what is important about them. You may wish to determine what kinds of prospects are the best customers, as Sugarman did. However, if you are using canvassing or department-store demonstrations to make sales, you'll have to devise some method for making the analysis—perhaps offering whatever you sell through several methods, dividing prospects into such classes as "department-store shoppers," "canvassed householders," etc.

Whatever you wish to test, you do so by finding some means to *relate sales to the factor being tested.* If you test advertising, for example, you key your advertisements. Suppose you run the same advertisement in several different magazines. You assign a different "department number" in the address given in each magazine, so you can determine which advertisement produced the greatest number of orders or the greatest number of leads. Or you can test different prices to see what works best in that respect. For example, you may find that you get fifty orders at ten dollars and sixty orders at eight dollars. Obviously, it pays better to get fifty orders at ten dollars; dropping the price by two dollars does not produce enough added volume to be worth the price cutting. To your surprise, you often find that you actually sell more at ten dollars than you do at eight dollars! Illogical? Who says so? Only testing can tell you the truth, and our idea of what is logical may not measure up. In introducing a new product for which no market price has yet been established, it is generally wise to try at least three different prices to see which one the customers are most comfortable with.

You can key to test one advertisement against another (we'll go into this in more depth in a later chapter), or to test packaging, or to test a name, or to test almost any other variable.

One thing to bear in mind is this: You do not have to run a full-scale campaign to test the market. You are probably going to make mistakes; that's the way we learn. Alert people can learn as much from fifty-dollar mistakes as they do from thousand-dollar mistakes. Obviously, a test marketing must be on a large enough scale to give representative results—by mailing to 100 people you cannot project the results of a 500,000 piece mailing. But you can probably get adequate test results by mailing 5,000–15,000 pieces first, properly keyed. Running a department-store demonstration for a week, in two or three locations, should give you a good idea of how viable a full-scale campaign of this kind would be.

FEEDBACK

Feedback is a term originating in electronics, borrowed by psychologists, and now used widely in many places to refer to knowledge of results. It is used to effect improvement or, at least, changes that one hopes will be improvements. That is what testing should do—provide feedback to the marketer which enables him or her to make appropriate improvements. The plan for testing should anticipate the need for this feedback and provide the means for getting it. Without feedback, the testing is meaningless. The feedback must be more than "go" and "no go" to be useful. It must tell you more than whether the marketing plan works or does not work effectively. It should tell you exactly what is good and what is bad about your marketing so that you can continue doing what pays and stop doing what does not pay.

The problem with too simple a testing plan is this: Suppose you run a direct-mail campaign using three separate mailing lists, for testing purposes, and three different prices. How can you tell whether any given list produced good or bad results because it was a good or bad list, or whether the price was responsible for the good or bad results? Of course, you can't if you vary more than one thing at a time. To make comparative tests, you have to have the test samples exactly the same, or as nearly the same as possible, except for one item. Then the differences in results among the samples tell you how that one item—price, for example—affects the outcome.

WHAT TO TEST

Knowing what to test is important. It is surprising how often marketers will test trivial factors before getting a fix on the important factors. For example, let us suppose that you are running several advertisements for a new item. What is the most important thing to test here? Price? Headline? Body copy? Sales argument? Media? All are important but not necessarily for the first test. If the item is a new one, and there is no history of sales experience, the first thing to test is the public response. All the other factors—headlines, media, sales arguments, etc.—are totally meaningless if you do not yet know whether the public will accept the item. If the public at large is not interested at all, what difference can the other factors make? All they can do is to mislead you into believing that your copy is poor or your media selection is faulty, and you can waste a great deal of money conducting tests because your first tests focused on the wrong things!

HOW TO TEST MARKET
SOMETHING NEW

The first test marketing of something new is not a test of the item itself. It should be a test of the appeal of the item *as you present it*. Take careful note of that distinction. What you really want to test is (1) whether you can motivate your prospects to become interested in your offer and to buy, and (2) if so, what is the most effective motivator. For example, let us suppose that you wish to offer the world a new service: writing letters for people who hate to write letters. Here are some of the ways you might present this:

1. A straightforward offer to act as a public scribe, writing letters for anyone who wants letters written.
2. A service to compose those special letters, such as complaints, condolences, and appeals.
3. A service that provides special skill in writing letters of affection, using the client's ideas, but expressing them more gracefully and eloquently than he or she could—essentially an editing/rewriting function.

If you make three mailings or run three advertisements, each along the lines of the three examples here, you will soon learn whether there are enough people interested in the service at all to make it a viable idea. If so, which appeal produces the best results? By answering that question, you will know if you have a viable idea along at least one of these lines; then you can begin testing prices and other factors, such as copy and headlines.

In your initial test you are out to discover whether any of the three appeals works better than the other two, or if they all work about equally well. Sometimes only one of the alternatives works. In this case, suppose that most people do not see the usefulness of a letter-writing service, but do agree that they'd like help in composing difficult-to-write letters, and respond only sparsely to the third presentation. That means you've found your market: those people who have trouble composing letters for special situations. You now know that you have a viable idea. You know what the market is, and all that remains is to refine your service to bring you the best return. Further tests and experience will provide the feedback for that.

In a large sense, testing never ends. The shrewd entrepreneur will always analyze what is happening and try to use that analysis to improve the business situation.

SOME TYPICAL MISTAKES IN TESTING

Among the many trivial things that some people spend money to test are such items as styles of type, color of paper, effects of two- or three-color printing versus black-ink-only printing, and a great many other factors which can only be considered to be cosmetic. In a huge mailing of many thousands of pieces, the color of the paper or the use of two-color printing makes a slight difference statistically. Certainly, there are many counselors who insist that such things *do* make a significant difference. My own experience with these factors, at least on a small-to-medium-size scale of advertising and mailing, is that the differences are minuscule, if they exist at all. In my own experience, any improvement achieved in results through these measures has not been great enough to compensate for the added cost. What I have found to be *the real issue is the offer itself*, and *how the public responds to it*.

One lesson emerges: *Test it for yourself.* In my personal experience I have more than once done the "wrong" thing and profited by it, or done the "right" thing and lost money in doing so. No matter what experts advise, it is wise to test the proposition and see if it works for *you* as well as the expert says it does. The most reliable advice comes from those who say, "This is what I have done, and it has worked well for me. But you should try this out for yourself first before you sink a lot of money into it, and see how it works for you."

WHAT THE PLAN LOOKS LIKE

Don't be misled by all these suggestions into believing you must have formal, elaborate documents representing your marketing plan. In actuality, even fairly large organizations have rather informal marketing plans; only the really large corporations can afford the mountain of bureaucratic paper that large staffs generate before undertaking even a modest effort. In practice, your physical plan—the actual documents representing your marketing plan—can be quite simple and informal. What is important is that you know who the prospects are, what you think will motivate them to buy, how you will get your offer under their noses, how you will test your plan to see what is working, and why each element works or does not work. In fact, it is better to keep the paperwork to a minimum. Don't spend any more than you have to, especially at this early stage, when you are not yet sure what is going to work. Simply commit to paper, for the record, the essential elements, as a reminder and as a basis for recording results so that you can decide what has worked and what has not, and the degree to which those things that work show a profit.

To test the salability of the offer, you must make that offer unmistakably clear. This is no place for subtlety or modesty. Therefore, you must first understand what it is you're selling. For example, in selling subscriptions to a newsletter I called *Government Marketing News,* I first tried to sell up-to-date news about the federal market, written from a Washington, D.C., location. Originally, I thought that the allure of getting information from someone on the scene would be irresistible. In fact, I even suggested that subscribing to that newsletter was tantamount to having one's own representative in Washington!

It didn't fly. I sold some subscriptions to a few small firms, but not enough. The big firms didn't subscribe at all. Why should they? Most of the larger firms had their own reps in Washington; some even had offices there. What could I offer that was better?

After numerous experiments, I happened—almost in desperation I guess—to stress one of the features of the newsletter: a monthly how-to article on proposal writing. Suddenly, I began to get subscriptions from some of the more important companies, and it became obvious that it was the how-to focus that induced the response. In sum, I had finally discovered what the customer wanted: not news, but know-how for *winning* contracts.

I began to focus on that feature, although I continued to offer whatever news I thought useful to my readers. At least I now knew what my *offer* was: tips, strategies, and other know-how for winning contracts. I began to sharpen my entire package toward making that offer as persuasive and attractive as I could.

The main point is that you can't make your offer more attractive if it isn't attractive in the first place. You cannot sell something where there is no demand. Does that sound pretty obvious? Unfortunately, a great many marketers miss that very point. The first step in marketing is to *determine the demand,* and then decide what ways you can sell that product or service to benefit your customers.

One man I know of is a hypnotist. He runs advertisements in the local newspaper, offering hypnotic sessions which will help relieve headaches and other stress-induced ills. He has had reasonable success until recently, but his advertisements are not producing the results they once did. He doesn't know what to do about it. On the basis of his several years of success, he has demonstrated that his offer of relief from certain ills is a viable one, and that customers will respond to it. Nonetheless, that expected response has dropped sharply in recent months. What should he do?

Of course, one thing he can do is to expand his advertising. Currently, he uses local print media, but he hasn't tried the audiovisual media of radio or TV in his area. Also, he ought to test his offer and find out if it is his best offer. Perhaps he can focus his offer to help people stop smoking, which might prove attractive to certain prospects. Or he might teach hypnosis, since many people are interested in the art. In any case, my suggestion would be that he test his basic offer first, and see whether his current offer is the most attractive one he can make as described by the benefits it promises.

Selling men's clothing gives you a choice of offers. Consider what things a man might look for when he buys clothing. Greater prestige in his career field? Being more attractive to women? Enhancing his self-image as a man about town? As a macho figure? Running some kind of advertising or promotion testing various offers will tell you which is the most productive.

Once you know what offer suits the "felt need" best, you can work at strengthening that offer, making it more credible and attractive. When you do, you may get a surprise or two, as I did with my newsletter enterprise. Once I learned that my most attractive offer would be to help readers learn how to write proposals to win contracts, I set about finding ways to bring that benefit into sharper focus to make it more credible. I realized that if I simply made a promise to deliver information to help win contracts, I would get a certain number of sales automatically. The response would be in proportion to how convincing, how credible, my offer was. Some prospects would just take my word for it and would gamble that I could help them, but a great many more might say to themselves, "Who is this guy? What are his credentials? How do I know that he can help me? How do I know if he knows what he is talking about?"

Obviously, the more solid evidence I could present that I possessed the means to deliver what I promised, the better response I was likely to get. Since I happened to have the track record of success that qualified me as an expert in the field, I presented my curriculum vitae in my literature, with suitable apologies for boasting. Thus, in presenting my record of success in winning contracts, I even used the headline, "Maybe I'm just lucky . . . or maybe I know something that *you* should know. . . ." I finished that piece of copy with the remark that if it was only luck, it seemed to rub off on my subscribers.

When it worked, I realized that I was not only selling contract-winning know-how, but I was also selling my credentials.

Where the benefit depends on what the vendor of the product or service can do, the prospect buys on faith. If that is the case with you, it's something to test: whether or not the prospect will buy *you*.

If, in making this analysis, you come up with several benefits you believe to be attractive, test each separately. If you offer all of them at once, and the promotion or advertisement works, you'll have no way of knowing which of the promised benefits was most attractive and produced the best results in follow-up marketing.

Another item that requires testing is the *medium* by which you reach prospects. You can test newspaper advertising against direct mail or radio, or even one newspaper against another. Here again, you can get too ambitious for your pocketbook. Testing everything that can be tested is too expensive and is unnecessary. There are always inexpensive alternatives, and the purpose of testing is to avoid the financial disasters that result from being wrong. There is no purpose in taking a cure that is worse than the disease!

8

Conducting Tests

*We often discover that we "know" things that
simply are not so if we test rationally and with
an open mina.*

ASSUMPTIONS

All tests are based on assumptions. The first marketing assumption you
made was that your offer would be most appealing if it promised certain
benefits—health, wealth, love, happiness, pleasure, ego gratification,
and so forth. You are now going to test this assumption and find out how
valid it is.

A test is useful only if you know exactly what you are testing and
have some means for ensuring that the results represent a fair measure.
Therefore, when you test marketing promotions or advertisements, you
want to observe the following two principles:

1. The promotions or advertisements should be as nearly identical to each
   other as possible, *except for* the factor being tested.
2. The alternatives being tested cannot be too numerous, if results are to be
   useful. It is best to keep the alternatives to three or five, at most.

Keeping the advertisements or promotions identical, except for what is
actually being tested, means that the copy should be varied as far as the
promise is concerned, but otherwise the copy is kept identical in each
version. The other elements of price, media, test population, etc. must be
kept as similar to each other as possible. That is, if you are running newspaper advertisements, try to select newspapers reaching the same kinds
of readers (for example, use all country weeklies, all suburban weeklies,
all city dailies, etc.). Or, if you are using direct mail, try to use mailing lists
that are similar to each other. If radio spots are being used as the

113

medium, the same types of stations (in terms of programming and listeners) should be tested. What you will vary will be the copy, and even then only insofar as it is necessary to test each of three or more offers: the headlines and some of the body copy.

Later, if you wish to test different prices, the same philosophy applies: Make the advertisements and promotions as nearly identical as possible, changing only the price.

Only by keeping everything *except what you are testing* identical can you be sure that your test results mean something significant. The difference in response will be due to the difference in offers, price, mailing list, or whatever specific variation you have selected to test.

HOW LONG TO TEST

Testing never ends. Even after you have been through all your initial shakedowns and have a viable business going, you should continue to exercise close control over all marketing, key everything so that you always know what marketing effort produces what results, and maintain careful marketing records. Business is dynamic, not static: Competitors come and go with competitive products and services; public perceptions and public tastes change, as do economic conditions. When you are small and running things on a personal basis, you become aware of changes swiftly; but as your business grows and becomes more decentralized, you become more and more isolated from the details. For that reason, unless you take specific measures to prevent it, your business can undergo changes, such as a sharp drop in sales, without your becoming aware of it immediately. One purpose in testing is to remain constantly sensitive to such changes. Insensitivity to change is one factor that all but destroyed the once-powerful railroad industry. It's a fact of modern life that change is continual and, unfortunately, the *rate* of change is exponential. In simple terms, that means that change takes place faster and faster all the time. Where once a new product might last for twenty-five years or a business might continue virtually unchanged for fifty years, new products become obsolete in ten years or less today, and businesses that do not change will find themselves rapidly reaching total obsolescence. Consider: Only twenty-five years ago, electric typewriters were the exception, rather than the rule, in most offices. Today, the reverse is true. Not too long ago, xerographic copiers didn't exist, and the copiers that did were crude and not popular. Small electronic calculators were not yet on the market (an electromechanical calculator cost on the order of one thousand dollars or more!). The United States was still struggling to put up that first, grapefruit-sized artificial satellite. Computers were still huge equipment complexes that only governments and large corporations could afford. Now, all of that is changed.

WHAT TO MEASURE: PROFITS

Never lose sight of the need for profit in any business enterprise. An enterprise needs sales, of course, but the sales must be made at a profit. Therefore, it is important to know what it costs to get those sales. Cost is not the same thing your accountant means by *cost of sales* figures. The accountant refers to dollars received or dollars that have become receivable (depending on your accounting system) when he uses the term *sales,* and his *cost of sales* includes just about everything that belongs in the cost columns. What we refer to is what it costs you to actually get the order, in terms of marketing/sales costs.

Overall, the things to be recorded are all the statistics related to mounting and operating the marketing/sales campaign: where, what, and how much went into the effort; and where, what, and how much was realized by the effort, keyed to relate cause to effect.

Take a direct-mail campaign as an example. In a test of three different offers consisting of three mailling lists of one thousand names each, which are similar in types of people, geographical distribution, income levels, etc., the price will be the same and all the copy will be the same *except for* the headlines and specific benefits promised. Keying the package is easy. The literature includes an order blank. All we need do is place some clue on the order blank—an inconspicuous A, B, and C, or some minor change in the mailing address, such as "St." in one, "Street" in another, and "Str." in the third version to distinguish one mailing from another. Costs, too, are the same for each mailing—printing, postage, envelopes, handling. The difference is going to be in the number of orders or rate of response for each list. If we have done everything we should have done, we'll soon know which offer the prospects find most attractive.

Some might consider this to be a test of the advertising or promotional copy, and the same as testing the offer. In fact, it is *if* the difference in the copy represents a difference in what the offer promises to do for the buyer. On the other hand, some people testing advertising copy are not really testing different *offers,* but they are testing superficial differences in the copy—straight text versus illustrated text, serious versus humorous copy, soft sell versus hard sell, and so forth. The result is that you cannot really know whether the offer you are making is the most appealing one possible. If the test washes out, and the product or service doesn't sell well, you don't have many clues as to what was wrong—your copy *or* your offer. If first things are to come first, you must *test the offer first.* Later, if you think it advisable, you can test different kinds of copy to see if one "pulls" better than another.

What you learn from the results of a test and how you utilize the information can vary according to what your product or service is. If you are offering a single item at a single price, you wish only to know which test mailing produced the greatest number of orders. Your recording sheet might be as simple as this:

DATE MAILED	NO. PCS.	NO. ORDERS	DATE RECD	$$
12/9/78	5,000	18	12/29/78	$360
		22	1/3/79	440
		37	1/7/79	740
		77		$1,540

At some point, when you believe you have gotten back all or virtually all the orders that will come from that effort, you will run totals and calculate profits, cost per order, etc. In the above case, you would probably have spent approximately $1,250 for the mailing, and unless you have a large markup on the item you are selling, you would not be doing at all well on this promotion. However, the above probably cuts off much too soon: A direct-mail campaign is more likely to require at least six to ten weeks for all the returns, and an effective mailing piece ought to bring back 150 to 300 orders. But it is not the number of orders or the rate of response that counts, it's the dollar totals of profit. Among my own most profitable direct-mail campaigns have been some that returned orders at the rate of about 1.5 percent, or 75 orders for 5,000 pieces mailed out. Moreover, you will soon discover that there is a phenomenon some dealers refer to as "drag." This refers to the orders dribbling in for months, even years, after a mailing. Many people respond only after a lengthy lapse, and this I have found to be true for business-executive customers as well as for individual consumer.

Not all campaigns have that simple characteristic hypothesized above of a single order at a single price. Many marketing campaigns make offers such that orders can be of different sizes. In this case, your data-recording form must provide for that by having a column in which you record the size of the order—dollars received for each order or for each day's orders. In my newsletter campaign, since I was offering a subscription and three different manuals—all of which could be bought as a single package at a special package price, or bought individually— I ran several additional columns:

MANUALS   SUBS   PKGS $$

This enabled me to keep close track of what each mailing did, in terms of dollars received, rather than orders. Since the orders varied in size (the range was from about fifteen dollars to one hundred dollars), I also had a column for average size or order for each mailing.

I was interested not in the absolute number of orders, but in average *size* of orders and, more specifically, in income versus outgo. If each mailing cost me $1,250, for example, my concern was to get that back plus enough to make the whole enterprise worthwhile, whether that meant 75 orders or 150 orders. Obviously, 50 one-hundred-dollar orders represent a different proposition than 150 fifteen-dollar orders (a total of $5,000 versus $2,250)—more than a two-to-one difference.

By keeping detailed records, I learned many things. The earliest mailings produced results well in excess of those I got from later mailings in response percentage. At least part of the reason for that was I was skimming my mailings. Later, when I began to use the list without selecting any particular types of respondee from it, the response rate went down. However, at the same time, the average order size went up because I began to get a greater percentage of orders for the whole package at one hundred dollars each, so that my average order size went up from forty seven dollars to nearly sixty dollars. I attributed this to the fact that most software developers tend to be small companies, and when I quit skimming and mailed to everyone on the lists, I reached a larger percentage of large companies.

Ultimately, after I had mailed to the list for nearly two years, the response began to decline seriously. This was due, I believe, to having worn out the list—gotten orders from most of those listed who were likely to order—and partly to a general business slump that took place at that time. The mail-order business tends to be like that. If you are selling some specialty items for which there is no real repeat demand, and no one really needs more than one of these items, the mailing list will soon be exhausted. Once you have saturated your market, you must go on to a new line of items or services. It is always wise to come up with something likely to be of interest to your established customers, for your customer list is a proven profit-making mailing list.

Another reason to test is so you can determine as quickly as possible when your sales are declining. Knowing when it is time to make a change is important. Even if you are fortunate enough to market the new Hula Hoop or Pet Rock, once the peak has passed, it is quite easy to lose all the profits you made earlier by fruitless flogging of a dead horse. Products can become obsolescent for a variety of reasons, but most often they are the victims of technological improvement. For example, thirty years ago it was almost a necessity to have a good rooftop antenna for decent TV reception. It was relatively easy to sell antenna installations in those days, but technological developments (drastic improvements in the tuners in TV receivers) have made rooftop antennas less important. TV sets are now able to get good, snow-free pictures with indoor antennas alone; ergo, the need for antennas has declined.

WHY YOU ARE MEASURING: THE CORRECT ATTITUDE

What is to be measured is everything. The more data you can collect, the more accurately you can analyze causes and the more effectively you can plan remedial action. Bear in mind that the attitude with which you approach testing must be open. You must strive to test any theories and assumptions you have or just to research the market when you are not sure. In any case, your purpose in testing is to get answers to such questions as:

Which of several alternative offers do the prospects find most appealing?
What is the optimal price (most profitable overall)?
Which of several items/services moves best?
In which medium does your advertising work best?
Which version of the copy works best?
Which kinds of mailing lists work best?
How does print advertising compare with direct mail? With TV/radio? With other methods (e.g., trade shows)?

WHAT TO DO WITH COLLECTED DATA

Obviously, some of the answers you collect have an immediate, direct application: You use the answers to discontinue whatever is not working and expand activity in whatever is working well. The best use of the data is not always that simple to identify. In many cases, the most effective use you can make of the data is as a basis for *further* testing. For example, if you were testing newspaper advertisements versus direct-mail solicitations and found the newspaper medium producing better results, perhaps you ought to find out which newspapers or what kinds of newspapers (morning versus evening or urban versus rural) produce best. Or, if direct mail worked better for you, you may wish now to try several different kinds of mailing lists in a comparison test.

Many people make the mistake of assuming that because a campaign produces what appear to be satisfactory results—an acceptable profit or a 4 or 5 percent response—that it is time to plunge into the campaign on the basis of what is known. The fact is where a 4 to 5 percent response might be excellent in one situation, it is unacceptable in others. Even with a highly profitable campaign resulting from a 4 percent response, that response is unacceptable until the marketer has tested *all* reasonable alternatives and determined that 4 percent is the best that can be achieved. If you can get a 10 percent response and you settle for 5 percent, your marketing is a failure, even though it produces a profitable operation.

The goal of all market testing is not only to find a *viable* marketing approach and methodology, but to find the *best possible* marketing approach and methodology. For that reason alone, there can never be an end to testing, for it is always possible that a better result can be obtained. Therefore, the principle exists that careful data should be held permanently on all marketing, carefully analyzed, and ultimately used to *improve the next campaign.*

This applies to all marketing, even to exhibits and sales booths at trade shows. Every participation should result in data for the purpose of evaluating one marketing/sales-prospecting method against another, as well as to improve participation in future events of the same kind.

ANALYSIS OF RESULTS

An acquaintance once remarked ruefully that he had been caught speeding on a New Jersey highway and forced to pay a fifty-dollar fine. I said that I hoped he had learned something from the experience, and he agreed he had: He had learned not to get caught when he was speeding. Unfortunately, a great many people use that kind of logic in analyzing marketing test results.

There are a number of errors commonly made. The most common one is leaping to conclusions on scant evidence. I recently read a newsletter that reports some new findings about advertising. According to this account, readership increases when an ad "bleeds," that it is unaffected by position, that it is made more effective by using four-color process than by using greater size. The newsletter even claims that more people respond to color in ads than they did ten years or more ago. Presumably, this data was based on research of advertising results made without regard to the *basic message* or *offer* in the advertisement, which makes the data immediately suspect. How can one conclude that you can increase the readership of an advertisement by the costly expedient of making it a four-color ad? Or that the color will produce better results than increasing the size of the ad? Or better results than changing the basic offer, headline, or reason offered the prospect for being interested? Supporting the concept that the benefit to the buyer is the most influential factor in any buying decision, there is evidence that more and more people are deserting name brands in favor of lower-priced brands and generic items. In short, the economy has reached a state where price is becoming a prime consideration, which illustrates the point that markets change almost continually, and a critical part of marketing is keeping in touch and responding to new marketing trends.

Another recent study declares that over 70 percent of those polled confessed that advertising was a great influence in their evaluation of products and buying decisions, with by far the greater portion crediting newspaper advertising with being the chief medium of influence, magazine ads second, and TV and radio following in last place.

Does this mean that these are universal trends? Certainly not, and anyone using this information to make marketing and advertising decisions is well advised to move ahead with caution and verify that these numbers apply to his own case. How accurately these trends reflect consumer influences in lines other than the one tested is totally uncertain. If this were not true, it would be unnecessary to do any test marketing of your own: You could base all your decisions on such reports. The fact is that such data ought to represent premises that you *might* use in test marketing to verify or disprove them for your own product or service.

In my case, once I had developed what appeared to be a reliable marketing formula, I did well with it for a number of months. Eventually it dried up and reached a point where the returns were not worth the investment and labor. At that point, it was time to start trying out other ideas and gathering new data. The fact that the formula was not paying was *all* I needed to know. Nothing lasts forever, and careful recording and study of marketing *results* tells you when change is due, when to cut your losses and go on to fresh efforts such as a new offer, a new package, promotional idea, or whatever you have been developing as a backup.

Expect the day to come when your campaign no longer pays, for whatever reason. It may do well for a number of years—some outstanding promotions or advertisements have been profitable for as long as forty years—or it may peak and decline rapidly after a few months. It's nearly impossible to gauge the life of a profitable campaign with any certainty. However, it is possible to keep your finger on its pulse by treating all marketing as *test* marketing: recording, measuring, studying, and evaluating results continually. It is thereby possible to detect a decline in campaign success and to discriminate between a temporary dip and a real decline. Ideally, you should be doing some of this test marketing *before* the decline occurs, and be prepared to shift gears rapidly when it becomes necessary to shut off the current campaign and move on to a new one.

The point is simple: The purpose of testing and gathering data is to keep your business healthy by furnishing you reliable data for decision making. Your marketing decisions should not be gambles based on hunches. They can be and should be based on solid data, properly gathered in continual marketing efforts.

9

Keying Advertising to the Market

*Most products and services sold lend themselves
best to one or another of the many possible
appeals. Smart advertisers do not try to force-fit
an appeal to fear, when the product is a
natural fit to an appeal for gains.*

Writing advertising and sales copy implements what has been empha-
sized in previous pages: focusing the appeal on what the prospect wants.
Your job as marketer is to persuade the prospect to want what you
promise more than he wants to keep his money. Those who like to create
clever little acronyms say that it's a matter of "AIDA," which in this case
refers not to the name of a Verdi opera, but this:

A = Attention
I = Interest
D = Desire
A = Action

What all this means is that an advertisement or a sales presentation
must be designed to get attention, arouse interest, generate desire, and
call for action.

That handy little acronym explains in general terms what an
advertisement or sales presentation needs to *do* if it is to be successful.
However, there is another side to this: what an advertisement or sales
presentation needs to *be* to be successful. Since making my message clear
is more important to me than creating clever acronyms, here is what
your advertisement or sales message must *be*:

1. A promise of some much-to-be-desired result.
2. An explanation of why/how that result will be achieved.
3. Some proof—or at least some *evidence*—that the result will happen.
4. A close—an instruction to the prospect to place the order.

Now let's combine these two approaches to how advertising and sales messages work, and see how they match up and what they mean in practical terms.

All sales appeals are based on promises. In the final analysis, the customer is buying a promise, and the success of the copy depends on how appealing the promise is and how effectively it convinces him that the advertiser can deliver on the promise. Let's consider what promises are appealing and what kinds are not, versus the idea getting attention and not getting it.

Obviously, you must get a prospect's attention before you can deliver your main message. In most advertising and sales situations you are competing for the prospect's attention. You are competing with other advertisers and sellers, and you are competing with other influences, as well. For example, in a print ad in a newspaper or magazine, besides competing with other ads, you are competing with the stories and articles, which are usually the reader's primary purpose in reading the publication.

Of course, there are exceptions to this. There are some cases in which the advertisements are the principal attraction of the publication. For example, in one magazine directed to purchasing agents in government organizations, the main attraction is the ads since the purchasing agents' chief interest is in reading what is being offered for sale. On the other hand, there are those who maintain that a half-page or quarter-page advertisement is more effective than a full-page advertisement simply because the editorial copy on the page draws readers to the page in the first place.

Assuming that the latter has some validity, the message to be drawn from it is this: If you plan a full-page advertisement, recognize that the advertisement is *entirely on its own* in attracting attention, as there is no story sharing the page to draw readers to it. Therefore, the advertisement itself must somehow be strong enough to attract readership. This might be accomplished with a compelling headline, some attention-demanding illustration, or in some other manner—but it must be accomplished, or the advertising budget is completely wasted. Without such expensive displays, it behooves you to examine the promise in your ad copy (whether it is a device, a system, a procedure, a job, or a service) and draw some commonsense decisions about it, such as What is it supposed to do? How well does it do it? What else would do that? Apply the method to advertising copy generally: What should advertising *do* for you? You must arrive at three answers:

1. Let people know *what* you have to offer.
2. Tell them *why* the product or service is good and what it can do for them.
3. Tell them *how* your product/service is better than your competition.

In some cases, the mere announcement that what you offer is readily available is sufficient to bring customers to your door. For example, suppose you have opened up a lunchroom or carryout service in an office building. The announcement itself may be enough to bring in some business, perhaps as much as you can handle, and you may need to advertise no more than that.

You may be one of those fortunate few. If so, you would be foolish to spend a great deal of money advertising. There are a number of rather inexpensive ways to make that bare-bones announcement of services:

- Distribute circulars.
- Make brief spot announcements on radio and TV.
- Run small advertisements in local print media.
- Use billboards.
- Put signs in your window.

Distributing circulars is usually the cheapest way to get the word out, and there are several ways to do that:

- Place them under windshield wipers of automobiles parked on large parking lots.
- Stick them under doors of private residences.
- Distribute them in office buildings.
- Mail them to residents in appropriate neighborhoods.

However, in most cases you will not be lucky enough to just announce yourself: You will have to do more than merely offer to sell your goods or services to customers; you will have to *persuade* customers to buy from you, and that kind of advertising will usually prove more expensive. If your product or service is something new in the market, you will have to explain what it is and why the prospect ought to try it; in sum, describe what it will *do* for the prospect. If the product is already well known—a TV set or dishwasher detergent—you will have to inform the prospect why he is better off buying from you than from competitors. Either way, your advertising argument must give the prospect *reasons* for buying. The prospect does not buy to please you, but to gain some benefit for himself, and the job of advertising is to make the prospect want to buy whatever you are selling.

MOTIVATIONAL FACTORS IN COPY

Prospects are motivated primarily by their own perceptions of the promised benefits and the desirability of the benefits. The chief difficulty for the advertiser is viewing the situation through the prospect's eyes.

The advertiser is trying to project what he believes will be motivating and credible. For example, a small advertisement in a current issue of *Salesman's Opportunity* magazine offers a free sample of Arizona bee pollen to anyone who writes and asks for it. Perhaps there are readers who know what bee pollen is and who will write for a free sample. However, the advertisement obviously has no appeal for anyone except the curious. On the other hand, another advertisement offers free samples of a product which, the advertiser promises, will dry clean any garment for ten cents, and the advertisement makes it clear that the advertiser's purpose is to find distributors or salespeople for the product. The principal motivator in the latter advertisement is a way to earn money, with a free sample of the product as the immediate inducement to respond and inquire further. The former advertisement offers nothing of benefit except free bee pollen. This is bad copy.

Note that the offer of a free sample is not only an excellent inducement to respond—it will give the advertiser a chance to send the inquirer a bundle of sales literature by mail—but that free-sample offer is also a factor in establishing credibility. In effect, the advertiser is saying, "Don't just take my word for this. Make me prove it. I'll send you a sample; you try this product out and see for yourself that it does what I say it does."

LANGUAGE IN MOTIVATION

Language is a critical factor in advertising. The words bee pollen, for example, mean nothing to me. Perhaps they are not intended for me. Perhaps the term has meaning only for certain individuals who are connected with agriculture. If that is so, *Salesman's Opportunity* magazine is the wrong place to advertise it. I am probably typical of the readers of that monthly trade paper of the sales and marketing world, and if an advertisement is incomprehensible to me, it is almost surely incomprehensible to a large proportion of readers. Even if I should be interested in Arizona bee pollen, I am not because I don't know what it is to be used for.

On the other hand, I do know what *dry cleaning* means, and whether or not the product actually performs, I get the idea. I won't send for the free sample because there is no way I could fit selling such a product into any of my activities. However, if the product fit into my scheme of things, I would be very much attracted to sending for a free sample and looking over the proposition.

Many words are highly motivational and never seem to lose their appeal. For example, a Carpet Barn in a metropolitan area runs a perpetual sale. Every week, without fail, the firm urges local TV viewers to take advantage of the week's special sale. The advertising strategy must be effective since the firm goes on repeating the message week after week, month after month, as well as regularly opening additional outlet stores. The public never gets tired of wanting to believe in the "special sale" and the promised savings. Thereby hangs a basic message of great importance in sales and advertising: People will gladly believe what they want to believe, whether or not it makes good sense. That is, most people are able to overcome their own good judgment if they want to believe something badly enough.

Clearly, if one wishes to employ good sense, something that is available every week, month after month and year after year, cannot be anything special. Nor can it even be a sale if it is a permanent sale fixture, but because such words as *sale, special sale, free, bargain,* and other such terms are so appealing, many people are easily able to persuade themselves to believe them. They *want* to believe them, so they do.

There are many other surefire terms. One advertiser has been running dozens of brief classified advertisements every month for a few years, with the brief introductory headline "PLASTERCRAFT!!! PROF-ITABLE HOME BUSINESS." The rest of the brief advertisement simply announces that molds are available and provides a name and address from which to get details. Meanwhile, another classified advertisement which has run successfully for many years is one that promises 400 percent profit for selling books by mail; it also provides a name and address for more information.

One reason such advertisements work well is because they use such words as *profit* and *profitable,* and they run under such advertising headings as *business opportunities* and *money-making opportunities.* Those are words people *want* to believe in.

AMBITIONS AND PROBLEMS

Most people have dreams, and many successful advertising campaigns exploit and take advantage of those dreams. For example, a great many individuals have ambitions to be successful authors, and many enterprises are based on that ambition. There are any number of individuals who advertise services to help the neophyte writer attain success through coaching, editing, or other services. There are also vanity presses, printers who offer to publish the aspirant's book for a fee, and there are still others who offer to teach the aspirant how to publish his or her own work—for some monetary consideration, of course. By the same token, there are schools that promise to help subscribers become successful artists, draftsmen, technicians, engineers, and accountants, or acquire other professional skills and abilities.

Note how these promises are structured: The smart advertiser does not offer to teach the aspirant how to write, but how to become a successful author; not how to clean furniture and rugs, but how to build a high income and retire well fixed; not how to set up and keep books, but how to be a successful accountant. The promise is usually tailored toward making some dream come true.

Another approach is to offer to solve some common problem. One quite famous and successful campaign of some years ago was run by a music teacher with the headline, "They laughed when I sat down, but when I started to play . . ." This campaign addressed the problem of timid people who found themselves wallflowers at social gatherings, but who dreamed of being the life of the party. The advertisements promised to make the prospects accomplished pianists, and it was a highly successful campaign.

Some people believe that the major problem in their careers is that they don't possess a college degree. Thus, there are many advertisements offering the prospect help in winning a college degree. The illustrations of this approach are numerous. The more common the problem, the greater the number of people who will notice and respond to such an advertising lure.

Therefore, the selling power of the promise made in your advertisement is partly dependent on the credibility structured into your copy, but largely due to the prospect's own desire to believe the promise. Thus, the greater the latter factor, the less need to build credibility arguments into advertising copy.

BUILDING CREDIBILITY WHEN IT IS NEEDED

Unfortunately, not every offer can promise a result that prospects are eager to believe. Most of the time, it is necessary to present a sales argument to make the promise credible. A female prospect would like to believe that Joe's Vanishing Cream will give her velvety skin and make her irresistibly beautiful, but she needs a bit of logical persuasion to be convinced. She is sophisticated enough to feel the need for some *evidence* so that she can rationalize her acceptance of the promise that the vanishing cream will work.

In short, an advertisement, like any other sales presentation, must make a promise and present evidence that backs up the promise to make it credible. There are many kinds of evidence, just as there are many kinds of promises.

USING EVIDENCE IN ADVERTISING

What is acceptable as evidence in advertisements does not have to meet the same requirements as evidence in a court of law. In a court of law, if one attorney brings in an expert to express an opinion, the other side has the right to challenge the expert's credentials. However, in an advertisement the "expert" may not be a bona fide expert at all, but an actor playing the part of a doctor or scientist. The viewer knows that the "expert" is an actor, yet the simulation is accepted as evidence.

Levels of credibility can be built by the use of such "experts" narrating the technical explanations and claims of the product. The requisite expert testimony may be written into copy, dramatized, or involve the use of a celebrity to lend credibility (as well as getting attention) to the product or service being advertised. Some advertisers even go so far as to offer as evidence of a product or service's claims a government certificate of some kind which purports to guarantee something about the product, whether germane to the promise or not. If that is not possible, an official-looking certificate may be produced that appears to originate from a professional testing laboratory or some equally impressive source.

For example, I recall an idea along these lines used to advertise a book on investments. The publisher ran a little certificate in his full-page advertising, carrying a border resembling a stock certificate, with notarized signatures, attesting to the truth of the author's assets. Just what that had to do with the promise being made in the book advertisement was not clear, but it lent a high degree of credibility to the book, and even appeared to be a guarantee of the book's validity as a good source for sound investment advice.

This is called authority evidence: the assurance of those who appear to be authorities of one sort or another that a claim is valid. There are at least two others kinds of evidence: peer evidence, which is like authority evidence except that it consists of the testimonials and assurances of everyday consumer-users that the product or service is what the advertiser says it is; and logical evidence, which is the persuasion of your own senses, once you understand the logic of why the service or product must inescapably be everything the advertiser says it is.

Currently, one cold remedy claims it is "indisputably" superior to its competitors because of the logical evidence. In this ad, a chart demonstrates that the two competitors relieve only six of twelve cold symptoms, whereas the advertiser's product relieves all twelve.

Of course, there is not a great deal of difference among all the leading brands in most product lines, and it is nearly impossible to maintain a marked technical superiority in most products today. In most cases, the leading products are like identical silver dollars. The advertiser's task is to prove that one silver dollar is better than another. For the most part, advertising success comes down to the proposition of what copy will most effectively influence the target population of readers, listeners, or viewers. What arguments, words, phrases, techniques, gimmicks, or devices will persuade people to buy what is offered? Persuading people to *buy* is what is essential, whether or not they are persuaded to believe.

In the advertising world it is generally assumed that if a prospect can be persuaded to believe, buying will follow automatically. Conversely, it follows that if a prospect is not persuaded to believe, he won't buy. However, that proposition has never been proven. No one truly knows what the relationship is between what the buyer believes and how the buyer behaves.

Moreover, some buyers have brand loyalty, and only a major persuasive argument will cause them to switch brands. Another buyer may be indifferent to brand names and will buy whatever comes quickly to hand, or whatever is cheapest or discounted. For these kinds of buyers, most advertising is wasted, yet even for those who have no brand loyalty, advertising can be important simply because many buyers will believe that anything not heavily advertised must be an off brand or otherwise unacceptable. To some degree, buyers in this society have become conditioned to believe that any product worthy of attention has to be advertised. Thus, "I never heard of it" can be a death knell for a product. It is by no means well established that what an advertisement says about a product is the sole influence on how buyers will react to it. Still, advertisers must proceed on the premise that prospects will know only what advertisers choose to tell them. To avoid advertising altogether is, perforce, an abdication of the marketplace to the competition. In other words, no one ever won the race by not trying to win.

FINDING OUT WHAT MATTERS TO A CUSTOMER

Frequently, the success of an advertisement, or of an entire advertising and marketing campaign, is the result of how well the advertiser has evaluated his customers' primary concerns. For example, take the case of a print shop located in a typical downtown business district. For most small print shops located in retail storefronts, there will be some individual consumers who come in off the street to have small jobs prepared. But by and large the print shop is going to have to depend on other commercial businesses for survival, since only businesses use printing services with some degree of regularity and in quantity. Thus, the print-shop proprietor will have organized his shop for either short-run or long-run printing jobs. Each requires an entirely different configuration of labor and equipment. Therefore, a well-run print shop performs one or the other, not both services. This decision should have been made when designing the shop itself, with a view to what kind of business the proprietor expects to pursue.

This example illustrates something too often overlooked in marketing: The marketer's perception is not important in advertising and selling; the customer's perception is the one that counts. Therefore, a marketing campaign designed to solicit new business must be tailored to fit the business design of the concern. Only in this way can the advertising get the proper message across to the proper prospect. Words in advertising are not effective if they don't convey to the prospect precisely what they mean to the proprietor. In sum, you cannot sell apples by advertising oranges!

Advertising copy can be further refined by being *specific*. For example, instead of advertising "speedy" service for a short-run print shop, try "eight-hour service," or whatever period of time you mean by that word *speedy*. Try, "Leave it in the morning; pick it up in the evening" because it paints a highly specific image and *suggests* to the prospect a *convenient* way to get the job done satisfactorily in the shortest possible time.

OTHER ADVERTISING MOTIVATORS: CONVENIENCE

Convenience is a remarkably effective motivator. With all the complaints about high prices, lower prices are far less effective a motivator, in many situations, than the conveniences offered. In many areas today, "bag and box" stores offering lower prices for groceries in no-frills surroundings have not done as well as expected when they first appeared. The public obviously wants low prices *without* giving up check-cashing privileges, bagging, and other conveniences found in the large food supermarkets. In the "cents off" type markets, service is almost totally self-service. Almost all such stores that have managed to survive have been located in the low-income neighborhoods where the inflationary pressures are the greatest.

Thus, many businesses based entirely on the convenience factor survive and prosper even in times of economic difficulties. Stroll through any shopping mall for an object lesson in this. In most malls, the small shops prosper on the overflow traffic from the large department stores that anchor most shopping centers. People prefer the greater convenience and service of the small shop to the crowded indifference of the department store.

Furthermore, businesses can offer credit terms by signing up with VISA and MasterCard banks. For many years, department stores attracted a great deal of their trade by offering charge plates as a standard convenience long before the modern credit card was introduced. This was not only a convenience for customers in the days before the personal checking account became a standard means for paying cash, but it facilitated returning unsatisfactory merchandise by giving the customer leverage in the event of a dispute with the store. Consequently, department store prices tended to be higher than those offered by many smaller stores until the advent of the bank charge cards. For a great many people, the conveniences made it worth the extra price. Convenience of credit is clearly an important marketing concept.

Moreover, one of the main attractions of mall shopping itself is its geographical convenience. Customers can browse, stroll in enclosed areas, and find plenty of parking space.

On the other hand, for some shopping by mail offers attractive benefits. Some mail-order entrepreneurs stress the convenience of shopping in your own home, but that is only one asset. Many people like browsing through catalogs, such as many mail-order firms offer. Today major mail-order firms offer several other convenience factors, such as accepting credit cards and/or having their own credit system, offering free trial periods and guaranteeing credits and refunds, and otherwise making ordering by mail appear an attractive way of shopping.

The mistake many merchants make in their advertising is to assume that customers perceive these convenience factors as bonuses. Unfortunately, they are not as obvious as we would like to believe, and it is essential that they be pointed out to the prospect if you want him or her to appreciate the convenience and be *motivated* by it. Be specific in your advertising about the conveniences offered, so the customer can appreciate and be motivated by them. If you're selling small-store service, remind the prospect how fatiguing and unpleasant it is to stand in long checkout lines and fight the way through crowded aisles. When selling the convenience of shopping by mail, stress the down side of store shopping; it's far more motivating than the up side of mail-order shopping. When selling the convenience of mall shopping, stress all the various conveniences one-stop shopping, parking, and credit can offer.

OTHER MOTIVATORS:
FEAR AND GREED

If you study enough advertising headlines, you'll soon see that they generally fall into one of two categories. Some appeal to the desire to *gain* something, which I refer to as *positive* motivation, or they appeal to the desire to *avoid* something, which I refer to as *negative* motivation. Both types of motivation are powerful, but some situations lend themselves better to the *fear* motivation (avoiding something), while others are better suited to *greed* motivation (gaining something). Let's consider a few typical cases and what kind of motivation is generally used by advertisers in each case:

Item Offered	*Motivation*
Insurance	Negative—don't leave loved ones unprotected in event of death, fire, or other disaster.
Cosmetics	Positive—be beautiful, young, attractive: outshine rivals.
Laundry detergents	Positive—have white laundry, be proud, be admired by others. But negative works also: Avoid embarrassment of gray laundry and "ring around the collar."
Investments	Negative *and* positive (fear *and* greed), the perfect combination—fear of being wiped out by inflation and economic chaos, with greed appealed to by the promise of great gains.
Automobiles	Primarily positive—the macho image, luxury, admiration of friends, and—lately—fuel economy. Negative is rarely used—that is, safety features are not usually stressed because it casts negative image over driving, and Detroit is reasonably sure that it isn't good practice to remind the public, even obliquely, about the enormous carnage on the highways.
News and business magazines	Mostly positive—be in the know, be successful (you have to be well informed to be successful).
Beer	Positive—fun with your friends, male and female.
Toothpaste	Mostly negative—avoid cavities and other tooth troubles, avoid bad breath (suggested indirectly, delicately).
Air travel	Positive—fun, entertainment, vacations, travel; like automobiles, avoid the subject of safety: dangerous ground to tread on, with many people nervous about air travel; difficult to use negative appeals effectively.
Train travel	Positive—comfort, relaxation. Few commercials or advertisements take full advantage of possibilities to use negative appeals regarding air travel with its crowded airports, lost luggage, and other associated problems
Drugs and medicines	Mostly negative, aimed at avoiding alleged shortcomings of competitive products, but with some positive aspects in extolling virtues of product being plugged.

As you can see from even these few examples, some items lend themselves better to one kind of appeal than to the other; and some are sold through hybrid approaches, having both positive and negative aspects. At the same time, there are some cases where there is little that can be employed as a positive or a negative argument. The advertiser has little choice. Let's consider some of the tabulated items and discuss the alternatives.

Insurance

It's almost unavoidable that an insurance advertiser must be primarily negative in selling insurance. It's inherent in that insurance is sold to counteract disaster. There are some positive things that could be argued, such as using certain types of insurance plans to save money or set up a retirement annuity, but those are comparatively weak arguments since most people are aware that there are better ways to invest or save money.

Guilt, too, is used in selling insurance. The typical insurance sales argument suggests strongly that anyone who has not protected his family is a reprehensible character. On balance, the nature of the product dictates how it must be sold.

Cosmetics

Here, again, the product all but impels the sales argument. The typical customer uses cosmetics to enhance his or her personal appeal. Most assuredly, negative arguments can be found, such as one that suggests that its products will help conceal skin blemishes, but by and large, people who buy cosmetics do so in the hope of *gaining* something, rather than avoiding or preventing something.

Laundry Detergents

Anyone who watches television commercials is conscious of the positive appeals and demonstrations showing the various products working their particular magic. Negative appeals will work here, too, and have been most effective for some advertisers, but the trend is distinctly in favor of positive appeals. Note how these have been used in selling dishwasher detergents, too, promising housewives that they will gain the admiration of friends and relatives for their sparkling dishes and glasses. Nevertheless, at least one dishwasher detergent advertises negatively by warning consumers that other detergents will produce water spots.

Investments

The gloom-and-doom writers of the past few years have found the perfect formula: fear *and* greed. Their arguments run that economic disaster lies ahead, but that it is possible to avoid financial disaster, and prosper and profit from the fiscal chaos itself. Even prestigious investment houses use the same combination of arguments.

Automobiles

Automobile manufacturers and dealers rarely make references to the safety features on their automobiles. The reason is that automobile travel has been anything but safe from its beginning, and the public is well aware of it. Therefore, it is a taboo subject, and discussing it even indirectly by reference to automotive safety features is hazardous to sales. Mention disc brakes, if it's necessary, but don't dwell on them. Proceed swiftly to luxury upholstery, colors, fast getaway, computerized ignition systems, and a hundred other technological wonders.

Airlines

The same considerations apply to advertising airline travel. Stressing how safe flying is, compared to automobile travel, is valid enough, but it would be a serious advertising blunder; so the stress is placed on the convenience and fun of the destination.

PRICE AS A MOTIVATOR

Among customers for whom price is a strong motivating factor, the extremes range from those who will almost invariably buy the lowest-priced item of its kind to those who deliberately seek out the highest-priced item. The motive of the low-price seeker is obvious, but even among the customers motivated entirely or at least primarily by low price, there are subgroups—each with a slightly different reason for seeking the lowest possible price.

There are those who believe that they cannot afford anything but the lowest-priced specimen of a given item, regardless of how they actually feel about price versus quality. Some of these buyers may even feel slightly underprivileged, but they strongly believe that they have no choice. There is another group that believes there is no significant difference among the various brands and models of any given item. They feel, therefore, that they are being cheated with higher prices or are paying for advertising when they buy. Some of these buyers may even believe that they are outsmarting the manufacturers who are trying to exploit them. Finally, there are some buyers who will buy the lowest-priced items on some lines, but not in all. For example, one buyer may believe that when it comes to clothing, he must seek quality; but when it comes to food, he seeks economy. In fact, a surprisingly large number of consumers will buy "only the best" in some things, while they pinch pennies on other kinds of things.

Most of the rest of the buying public avoids these extremes, but almost everyone fits into the third category, sometimes being motivated by price. One reason price motivates buyers is because for many, price is the only factor by which they are able to judge the value of an item. Take a can of soup, for example. For many, the safe course is to buy the name brand—that is, the brand that has become familiar through extensive and continued advertising. Nonetheless, there are some buyers who are unimpressed by names or advertising presence, and they will try to make a value judgment on other bases, such as personal pride and visibility. For some buyers, what others think is of utmost importance. Thus, some will buy strictly on the basis of the lowest price when the items involved are those that no one else will see. However, where clothes, appliances, furniture, or anything else that is highly visible is involved, pride compels this buyer to buy "the best."

Pride is a powerful motivator, and many successful appeals are made on this basis. For some buyers it goes even beyond that and involves their self-esteem. That is, some people will pinch pennies in many other areas, but will spend more than they can afford on an automobile or clothes because it makes them feel good. In the final analysis, all pride is self-esteem, and the pursuit of prestige, the admiration and respect of others, is food for the soul. Never underestimate its power in motivating buyers.

PRICING TO MOTIVATE

Depending on the nature of what you are selling and the prospects you seek to reach, pricing too low can be as harmful to sales as pricing too high. From an advertising viewpoint, *stressing* low price can be as harmful as stressing factors that suggest the price is high. Typically, advertisers who offer what they believe to be a bargain stress the low price specifically, while those who are asking a high price generally stress quality and exclusivity, which are usually taken as code signals for high price. Then again, some advertisers try to have it both ways by claiming to offer the highest quality at the lowest prices—a claim that generally falls flat. Such a hybrid claim is self-defeating because it makes two claims which oppose and cancel out each other: The prospect who seeks high quality will be skeptical if the price is too low, and the prospect who seeks low price is wary of an item which is likely priced above the bargain-counter level.

The simple fact is that a price is only "too high" or "too low" with respect to a given class of customer. It is also true that you can't have it both ways: The advertiser must decide beforehand which customer he wishes to reach and motivate. Any effort to reach and motivate all buyers with the same appeal is doomed to failure. No advertisement can hope to bridge such a misguided pricing structure. For example, General Motors sells five different automobiles to five different kinds of customers: Each is organized as a separate company, with its own advertising and sales campaigns. The reasons should now be obvious.

A WORD ON INQUIRY ADVERTISING

The nature of *what* you are selling often dictates *how* you must sell it, and that in turn often dictates how you must advertise. For example, if you are selling big-tag items, you are primarily looking for sales leads, not orders, with your initial advertising. Therefore, you use inquiry advertising designed to *elicit inquiries* from interested prospects. You will then do whatever follow-up you have decided is appropriate to close the sale, such as a package of literature, a telephone call, or a personal visit.

The point is that advertising to get orders directly from the advertisements is either prohibitively costly or can't be done at all. This being the case, it would be foolish to spend more on advertising than is necessary to bring in the inquiries. In fact, many advertisers have a cost-per-inquiry standard, and they judge the effectiveness of their advertising by the cost per inquiry it represents. For example, a one-hundred-dollar advertisement that produces two hundred inquiries represents a fifty-cents-per-inquiry cost. That may be either too high a cost or entirely satisfactory (possibly even most gratifying) depending on the business.

You need not necessarily do your own inquiry advertising, either. There are numerous marketing services that will prepare your advertising and charge you a flat price per inquiry, which may run as little as twenty cents, or as high as several dollars per inquiry. Some of these are mailer services: You supply the copy containing your offer (e.g., an information brochure, a calendar, or some other item you offer as an inducement to the reader to respond), and the packaged mailer incorporates your offer as one of many other advertisements in a single mailing. Responses to your advertisement are then forwarded to you with a bill. From that point on, it is up to you do the follow-up and close the sale.

This method takes much of the risk out of the advertising investment because you pay only for results. Of course, it also has a down side in that you might have gotten your inquiries or leads at a far smaller cost per inquiry had you paid in full for the advertising, with the inquiries coming directly to you, instead of through such an advertising service.

Inquiry advertising is based on the idea that some number of those who see or hear your advertising will be motivated to want to learn more about what you offer and how your offer can be of benefit to them.

Remember that advertising is expensive, and inevitably a great deal of any advertising cost is wasted. There is no way to avoid that. The only perfect advertising would be advertising that reached the eyes and ears of only interested prospects, and that is impossible. There is no way to arrange things so that you pay only for the message that reaches interested prospects. So you undertake other measures, which, you hope, will at least reduce the waste.

One way is by careful selection of the media. If you are selling a newsletter or services connected with helping people in their investments, you'll want to advertise in such publications as the *Wall Street Journal* or, possibly, *Money* magazine. Obversely, you may reach a few investors by advertising in *Popular Mechanics*, but the percentage will be small and the waste great, so you would be unwise to advertise such an investment newsletter there.

If you wish to run inquiry advertising, certain considerations apply: Your offer must be such that it attracts inquiries from the proper prospects. It is quite easy to go astray and waste your advertising dollars attracting the wrong people. Even though you have selected a good medium, such as the *Wall Street Journal*, for your inquiry advertising directed at investors, not every reader of that paper is a good prospect for you; at least some of its readers are not investors. For example, should you offer, as an inducement to respond to your advertisement, a sample copy of your newsletter or a free special report on some matter of direct interest to investors, your advertisement ought to attract inquiries from qualified prospects. However, suppose you decide to increase the inducement by offering everyone who responds a handsome calendar. You may get a great many inquiries because a great many people would like a handsome free calendar, but you will probably waste a great deal of money sending calendars to inquirers who have no interest in investments or investment newsletters.

On the other hand, if you go to extremes in qualifying inquirers (if, for example, you offer only to supply subscription information, thereby restricting your response to only those with a direct interest in an investment newsletter), you will severely limit the response. You may get only a handful of inquiries, not enough to make the method worthwhile.

In general, most advertisers think that a 3 to 4 percent response to a direct-mail campaign is satisfactory, and they usually structure things so that such a response produces a reasonable profit. However, that is for cold selling. For selling to a better-qualified list, such as those who have responded to advertising and indicated an active interest, response rates and orders closed as high as 40 percent are not unknown, and an effective campaign ought to produce at least 10 percent.

10

How to Write Advertising and Sales Copy

Cleverness and cuteness in copy do not sell anything. Only clear communication and effective persuasion do. Don't embark on ego trips; sell the product.

ADVERTISING AGENCIES

The advertising business is a major industry in the United States today. The majority of the biggest agencies are located in New York City, with branch offices elsewhere. The large agency has a number of departments handling many functions. Basically, the functions of an advertising agency cover the development of advertising concepts, the creation of the advertisement, and the placing of the advertisement (buying space and time) among the media (newspapers, magazines, radio, TV, billboards, etc.). The typical agency has writers, artists, photographers, and buyers. Many of the larger ones also have their own studios for creating and taping TV commercials, so their staffs include technicians, directors, and other specialists for auditioning and selecting professional actors, actresses, models, and narrators.

Most of these services are *free* to the clients of these agencies if the client buys enough time and space to make it worthwhile. The agency performs all the space and time buying for the client, billing him at whatever rate is stipulated by the medium; the agency gets a 15 percent discount from that rate, which is the agency's profit. In addition, most billings allow an extra 2 percent for rapid payment—within ten days of the invoice—so that the agency can actually realize nearly 17 percent discount overall. So, while an agency may incur costs of $200,000 to prepare and manage a complete advertising campaign for a client, the client may well buy several million dollars' worth of time and space, on which the agency will realize a gross profit of from $150,000 to $167,000 for each million dollars spent.

Many of the larger agencies will not undertake campaigns for advertisers who are not going to buy a great deal of space/time because they simply are not set up for charging fees for their creative services. Furthermore, it's simply not profitable for them to handle a multiplicity of small accounts. The small advertiser who needs help in creating advertising copy must therefore turn elsewhere; there are several options.

- There are many small advertising agencies that offer advertising creative services on a fee basis for small businesses. Almost all cities have several listed in the Yellow Pages.
- Some of these agencies are not full-service advertising agencies, but graphic arts establishments of commercial artists that often have typesetting capabilities. These establishments usually do not have writers who specialize in advertising copy on staff, but they do have a roster of free-lancers on whom they call for assignments.
- There are free-lance copywriters who contract directly with clients and who can aid in finding a commercial art service or who may take on the whole creative job and subcontract art and whatever else is necessary.
- The advertiser may always do his own copywriting and hire an editor as well as a free-lance commercial artist for assistance.

COPYWRITING

The most basic rule for copywriting is also the most basic rule for writing in general: Don't be clever; be clear. Focus copy entirely on what you want the prospect to *understand*. Remember, you cannot make a reader understand something you do not understand yourself, so it is wise to go back and reread drafted copy for clarity. It's amazing to me how often poor copywriting consists of nothing more than a half-baked notion, instead of well thought out, original ideas.

A recent advertisement in a consumer magazine for hammers headlines a promise of "striking success." The juxtaposition is clever— hammers and "striking success," but experience has demonstrated that cleverness does not sell anything. Clever copywriting is self-indulgent, and it is not good salesmanship. A bit further on in the copy appears the promise that is expected to motivate the reader to become a buyer. It exhorts the reader to be a "super doer," because "super doers do more" with this offered hammer. The problem with this copy is that the appeal is well below the middle of the body of the copy. Only if the reader has read that far can the advertiser hope to win a sale.

The strategy doesn't make good copy sense. If the reader's attention and interest are to be aroused by the headline, *the basic promise should be in the headline*. The "super doer" line ought to be the headline of the advertisement. There is time enough to be clever later in the copy when it won't matter as much that cleverness doesn't sell anything.

Moreover, even the term "super doer" is not the clearest idea that could have been used. Something such as "Join the professionals: Use a professional hammer," might have been more to the point, for that is what the copy seems to be trying to say.

In another example, a headline on a full-page ad that appeared in a magazine addressed to small-business owners and executives promises that even if the reader is wealthy, the advertiser may "just keep" his family from becoming homeless. The advertiser? An insurance company, of course. The copy includes a photograph of a handsome suburban home with an automobile parked in the circular driveway, and a short block of text which elaborates on the theme of the headline. This is a good advertisement containing all the necessary elements: It identifies the reader for whom it's intended, and it furnishes a compelling reason to read the message in the copy.

Another advertisement is an inquiry advertisement by a national motel chain offering a road atlas and travel guide free if you stop at one of the chain's establishments, or you can send for it for a few dollars to cover postage and handling. A good advertisement, but it has some weaknesses. The headline urges all America to "turn in"—presumably at one of their motels. It is another example of clever self-indulgence by a copywriter, missing the mark. You still have to read the body copy to learn that the road atlas is offered free.

What this advertisement needed to fulfill its mission is a headline that says something like, "1983 Road Atlas/Travel Guide Free," and then goes on to expand on that idea in the copy.

HEADLINE/COPY/SALES STRATEGY

The basic sales strategy is always an emotional appeal—a promise of some much-to-be-desired result. The specific strategy of any advertising sales effort involves a decision as to what promise to make and how to back it up with evidence to make it believable. More importantly, there are two subordinate strategies making up the overall strategy: the strategy of the headline and the strategy of body copy. The two are most closely related yet distinct; each has its own job to do. Strategies must incorporate the following:

1. Overall advertising strategy—the general motivating approach or promise that will persuade the prospect to become your customer.
2. Headline strategy—the headline copy and/or illustration that will arrest the prospect's attention and arouse enough interest in the promise to permit you to deliver the remainder of the message.
3. Copy strategy—the information that will be accepted as proof or good evidence that the promise is valid.

INTRODUCING THE

INFLATION FIGHTER!

YOU CAN Make $500. — $1200. A Year — Selling BUSINESS CARDS From YOUR HOME!

THIS YEAR I will sell, from my home, a QUARTER MILLION Business Cards!

That is 250 orders of 1000 cards each at a $5. average profit per order — a yearly profit of $1250.00!

YOU CAN DO IT, TOO!! Your friends, neighbors, business and professional folks in YOUR HOME TOWN, buy and use Business Cards. YOU can offer LOWER PRICES than local printers, fast service, and guaranteed satisfaction!

SELLING BUSINESS CARDS FROM YOUR HOME . . . . .

1. A professional business of YOUR OWN!

2. A profitable work-at-home endeavor!

3. Repeat orders coming in automatically!

My Report: "HOW TO MAKE MONEY SELLING BUSINESS CARDS FROM YOUR HOME" is brand-NEW. . . copyrighted full instructions for you to make money in this home business. Follow the easy-to-read instructions: where and how to order business cards; how and where to advertise "PROFITABLY".

Follow my methods and you WILL make money! I know — I do it every day — and have for five years.

Wouldn't YOU invest $4. to make $500. to $1200. in just one year?

READ WHAT OTHERS SAY!

Each Letter kept in our files for verification

"Your Business Card manual is good. Never seen anything like it in my 30 years as a sideline mail order observer." Fred Otsuka, 20079 San Miguel Ave., #6, Castro Valley, CA 94546.

"Your Report, How to Make Money Selling Business Cards, is well-written and easily understood. Some Reports I have read are confusing to the beginner. Your Report is clear and straight to the point." E. B. Backerman, Box 837, Benton, Ark. 72015.

"Your Manual is easy to read and understand because of your straight-forward, logical-sequence, all-information style of writing, which I feel is very important in a "How To" book. The repro of your ad, sample of sales letter, order form, added much to this manual." Robert D. Fluharty, Box 627, South Windsor, Conn. 06074.

"Your excellent Report about selling business cards is well worth the $4. price." Peter Outerbridge, Mount Royal, Quebec, Canada.

"I enjoyed your report. I have read a great many folios and books, etc., but yours is one of the best and most complete." — Patricia Dayton, Publisher THE DOLLAR STRETCHER, 1907 Lincoln Ave., Mendota, IL 61342.

"Just finished reading your new manual. Your writing is comfortable and your line of reasoning is easy to follow. The information you give is clear and concise; your advice is good; the samples and exhibits are well displayed." Roy Wilcoxin, 3216 N. 80th Terr., Kansas City, KS 66109.

"Your report is interesting and well-written." Matt Dol, Ed. & Publisher, PO Box 626, Seabrook, MD 20801.

"Just read the first draft of your new Report. I was surprised at the completeness and the soundness of your program as presented. I would be interested in adding your new manual to the ones I am already selling." — Fred Morangelli, 3175 Brixton Lane, #2, Levittown, NY 11756.

"Your manual "HOW TO MAKE MONEY SELLING BUSINESS CARDS FROM YOUR HOME" is terrific! Anyone who applies himself to your easy-to-follow instructions can't help but succeed." Dorothy Tueller, Publisher, 7219 Promenade Drive, Salt Lake City, Utah 84121.

MAIL COUPON TODAY

TO: *PAUL K. ALEXANDER & ASSOCIATES*
14504 Lancia Circle, Chantilly, VA 22021

YES, I want to make extra money! Enclosed is $4. Rush my copy of your NEW REPORT by return mail, postpaid.

Name ____________________

Address ____________________

City, State & Zip ____________________

FIGURE 6. A typical mail-order advertisement for a product.

Here is an example to illustrate these principles. The advertiser believes that readers will react to the term "INFLATION FIGHTER!" because most of us are concerned with inflation today. The headline invokes and addresses a recognized and almost universal problem, which is a good basis with which to begin the advertisement. However, the headline is only a vague promise to help the reader because it doesn't indicate *how* the help will be forthcoming. There are at least two ways to fight inflation—by reducing costs and increasing income. Paul Alexander clarifies that promptly in his subhead: "YOU CAN Make $500–$1200 A Year—Selling Business Cards From YOUR HOME!"

Now the reader understands the entire basic proposition. The promise is to enable the reader to make from $500 to $1200 a year extra income working at home in a spare-time enterprise (by implication). The headline and subhead get all of that information across quite nicely. It's good headline strategy because it is based on a sound appeal and it addresses a common problem. It is perfectly clear what the reader is going to have to do to earn that extra money. Moreover, because most people shrink from selling—especially cold sales calls on total strangers—Alexander hastens to make it clear that it isn't necessary to leave home to accomplish the selling and earn extra money. If the advertiser had failed to make that clarification, a large percentage of readers would turn the page at once.

Alexander immediately begins to furnish evidence that what he is talking about offering is a legitimate proposition, that he knows what he is talking about, and that the reader can place confidence in his offer. He does this by first stating unequivocally that he does this himself, then he describes the ways in which he does it, assuring the reader that he can do it too. Finally the ad reproduces a number of testimonials.

Since I know Paul Alexander quite well, I can vouch for the legitimacy of what he says in this advertisement and verify that this advertisement is successful and does produce a satisfactory number of orders.

The next illustration is another one of Alexander's ads. This time a consulting service for local clients or by mail is advertised. The headline is posed as a question, a method commonly agreed upon by experienced advertising people as a good way of getting attention and arousing interest. Of course, the question must be germane to the promise. In this case, Alexander is addressing millions of people who aspire to small, at-home mail-order businesses. Alexander also knows that his question will be of interest to a great many people who read *Timely Tips* magazine, where the ad appeared, because it's that kind of publication with a focused appeal to would-be entrepreneurs.

He loses no time following up his headline with a subhead that elaborates on the message in the headline and fans the interest in the

FIGURE 7. A mail-order advertisement for a service.

copy. Note that he immediately assures the reader that he (Alexander) can help and launches into the benefit, which also embodies the major reason for reader interest. The benefit promised is triplefold: saving money, making money, and avoiding exploitation. The latter is a perfectly valid sales point, for a great many hopefuls are victimized every year by worthless schemes and misrepresentation. The headline strategy is a solid combination of "greed and fear" motivators, starting with a rhetorical question intended to provoke interest.

The strategy of his body copy is also quite sound and even sophisticated. Its overall tone is one of complete frankness, making no elaborate promises, which lends the copy a large measure of credibility. Alexander then goes on to reinforce his credentials with a brief biographical summary and the prestige of his teaching credentials.

Finally, Alexander does not ask for money, but invites the reader to write for a brochure, which is offered free. Therefore, it's an inquiry advertisement, because the consulting service is too costly to be sold from a half-page or even a full-page ad, and it is necessary to provide the prospect much more extensive reading matter and sales arguments.

Figure 8 illustrates another type of advertising. It's a brochure for a seminar I conducted, which was quite successful. There are a number of things to be noted about this brochure. First, the mechanical detail. The brochure was printed on 8½-by-11-inch paper and folded to fit into a number 10 envelope, together with a cover letter, and mailed first class. This alone is a radical departure from the way most organizations sell seminar attendance. Most prepare a large brochure—four or six pages, folded down to 8½-by-11-inch size and mailed without an envelope (self-mailer) at bulk rates. The result is that since it is obviously some kind of advertising, a great many are thrown out without being read, whereas this brochure was read because it arrived in a white business envelope under first-class postage.

Note the copy on the front panel, which is the equivalent of the headline in a print advertisement. First, it coins a new word—Proposalmanship—not a particularly brilliant coinage, of course, but something with a purpose, to be explained presently. Meanwhile, it's different and somewhat attention-getting, and because it's explained immediately, it is not cryptic.

Note that this is promised as a *graduate* course in the art of proposal writing—*advanced* information. The headline and subheads also stress the word *winning*, which strikes at the heart of proposal writing, because it's a highly competitive effort to win a contract for a great deal of money. The combination of the basic promise to teach the reader how to *win* through *advanced* methods in this *graduate* course, all but ensures that the reader will open the brochure and read on.

The basic strategy of that headline copy is to stress winning, which is the only reason anyone would attend such a seminar, but with the special twist that this is *different* from other seminars in that it is a *graduate* program, and that its focus is on contract-winning strategy (not proposal writing, as with most other seminars). To bear out the evidence that it is different, the whole mailing is done in a unique manner.

Opening the brochure to the first inside panel, the reader is offered an elaboration of the idea, starting with a repeat of the front-panel headline, this time with extra stress on the word *strategy,* and expanding on the explanations. Note that the significance of the coinage "Proposalmanship" is explained, and that the concept of contract-winning proposal strategies is repeatedly stressed, because that is the main theme of the entire seminar: how to develop a winning *strategy* in each proposal competition.

Figure 9 shows the second inside panel and a back panel. The main thrust of this copy is to authenticate the brochure's claims by demon-

"Proposalmanship"

The graduate course in

Winning
Government
Contracts

through

Strategy

**8:30 a.m. - 4:30 p.m.
January 9, 1979**

**Pennsylvania Room
Mayflower Hotel
Washington, D.C.**

Proposalmanship:

The Graduate Course in Winning Government Contracts— through STRATEGY

A fact-packed, one-day workshop that will graduate you from proposal writer to a *contract winner.*

In just one day, you'll receive the benefit of years of experience from government marketing experts who have won millions of dollars in contracts. And they did it by employing the proper strategies.

How to sell directly to the Government—"across the counter."

How to appear to be the low bidder—and how to win even when you're not the apparent low bidder.

How to make your proposal THE OUT-STANDING ONE.

How to analyze the requirement—identify the critical, key point on which award will hinge—develop a WINNING STRATEGY.

"Proposalmanship" is a word coined by Herman Holtz, President and founder of Government Marketing News, Inc., some years ago to dramatize the difference between "proposal writing" (which anyone can do) and the art of winning (which is another matter entirely).

Its essence is *strategy* — the strategy of programming, the strategy of presentation, the strategy of costing.

Its application depends upon complete and sound knowledge of Government procurement *and* contract administration, upon understanding of what the Government means when it issues a Request for Proposal — what the Government agency is looking for as a response to that request — and upon the art of marketing and salesmanship.

FIGURE 8. Seminar brochure for direct-mail promotion.

strating that the lecturer has the proper credentials, that other companies have sent participants, and that prior participants have found the
session most helpful.

The final panel (not reproduced here) contains an outline of the
day's program on one side and a registration form on the other. In the
program, the earlier themes are carried out; it lists the kinds of
information that would be imparted, including such choice delicacies as
"inside tips" and how to *appear* to be a low bidder even when not.

Thus, the strategy of the body copy was not only to provide
credibility factors, but also to stimulate desire by offering things ordinarily not available elsewhere—the many "insider tips"; several basic
strategies, such as a method for maximizing proposal technical scores
and ways of using the Freedom of Information Act to strengthen the
proposal; a special method for analyzing the customer's requirements;
shortcuts in production of the final proposal; tips on organizing and
leading the *ad hoc* team generally assembled for a proposal effort; and
numerous other tidbits.

There is a very sound principle underlying much of this, which is
itself an excellent basis for evolving advertising strategies. One of the
principal factors that facilitated the development of an unprecedentedly
successful seminar brochure was that the promises made and the
program offered addressed common problems. Almost everyone who
has ever had to produce a proposal for a sizable contract becomes
familiar with a number of typical problems. They can hardly fail to be
interested in any offer of help, since proposal writing is a critical sales
function in a great many companies.

Here are typical questions I asked myself: What are the typical
problems of those I wish to reach with this copy? What are the most
severe problems? The ones they recognize most quickly? The ones they
most desperately need solutions for?

Next: Which problems will my offer solve? How? Can I prove it?
How can I best dramatize the problem and the solution?

Finally: What else have I to offer? What other benefits, goodies—
and, *especially, things no one else can or has (at least) thought to offer?*

Advertising that addresses a common problem is immediately on
the right track *if* the advertising can offer a plausible, *believable* promise
to help solve the problem. Of course, there are other considerations.
The solution you offer must be *attainable* by your intended customers. A
five-thousand-dollar solution is of little value to someone who cannot
afford to buy it. Nor can a wage earner travel long distances to gain the
benefit you offer in a seminar.

Most importantly, if you do not have the personal experience to
discover the severe problems your offering solves, a bit of research is a
must. For example, although I personally knew the proposal-writing

Herman R. Holtz, President of Government Marketing News, Inc., is the author of more than $52 million worth of successful proposals. He conceived the strategies and, in most cases, managed the projects, most of them in professional services—training and other human resource development projects. He had earlier spent a number of years as an electronics engineer in defense and aerospace industries. Mr. Holtz has written widely on the subject of government marketing, founding Government Marketing News, Inc., and serving as marketing consultant to many companies. He has personally authored a number of training programs for different government agencies and has been a guest lecturer on federal procurement at the Civil Service Commission's Management Sciences Training Center.

What previous participants have said about GMNI's workshops.

"Case histories excellent, well done."

"Enjoyed the experiences and tactics of other contractors."

"I lilke what Mr. Holtz had to say about understanding government games and evaluating RFPs."

"I have found much useful reconfirmation and focus on the items."

"The sample request was a good exercise in dealing with what seems like the impossible."

"... thought provoking ..."

"... a good reminder of good proposal writing practices."

HANDOUT MATERIALS

It's a fast-paced day because there is so much to cover. You'll get a large package of materials to carry away, however, for your future reference, to refresh your memory on strategies, organizing and leading proposal efforts, and dozens of new ideas for your future proposals.

The Truth About Winning Government Contracts!

Have you heard that all bids you see in the CBD are wired? That it is futile to bid them? That you have to know someone to win? That you have to be a huge corporation to do business with the Government?

Myths, all of them (and other tales like them). Herman Holtz (founder and President of Government Marketing News, Inc.) has been proving that for years, over and over.

That's what led to these seminars: Holtz decided it was time to tell other Government marketers the truth—that these myths are the rationalizations of the losers, excuses for failure . . . alibis for being unable to write *superior* proposals, the kind that WIN.

Some of the organizations who have attended previous workshops on "Proposalmanship":

Systems & Applied Sciences Corp.
RAM Corporation
Pitney Bowes
Bionotics Corp.
Scope Electronics
Evaluation Technologies
Sikorsky Aircraft
Rehab Group, Inc.
U.S. Industries
Baker, Hames & Burkes Reporting, Inc.
General Kinetics, Inc.
Tracor Systems Technology Div.
Wapora, Inc.
Watkins-Johnson Co.
Analytic Services, Inc.
OFEGRO, Inc.
Interaction Research Institute
Bolt, Baranek & Newman, Inc.

FIGURE 9. Additional panels of seminar brochure.

business quite well and was familiar with most of the problems entailed, I knew nothing of seminar production and promotion. I did several things about this: I made it my business to get on various mailing lists to gather seminar brochures for study. I asked friends and business acquaintances questions. I attended a number of seminars, and I got myself invited to be a guest speaker at a number of them. By the time I had done all this, I had a rather good idea what the problems of running seminars were and what kinds of questions attendees have in mind when considering whether or not to attend one.

It was partly on the basis of this information that I decided my seminar had to be a "graduate" course; that it had to deal with strategic concepts in proposal development, rather than basic principles and mechanics; and that it had to be promoted in a different way.

Moreover, I followed a similar path in establishing my own mail-order enterprise. I ordered many different mail-order "plans" and textbooks, talked to a number of other mail-order entrepreneurs, read newsletters and other publications in the field, and did some small-scale experimentation. I decided that what I could do best was develop the sale of reports on subjects related to helping others launch their own business enterprises. I thought back to many of my own problems in getting a small business started and checked around to see how common these problems were. When I found such a problem, I developed a report, explaining how I overcame or solved the problem. Most of these reports sold quite well for the obvious reason that each satisfied a known need.

THE UNIQUE SELLING POINT

A prominent advertising agency executive in New York has explained that his basic approach to advertising is to find a "USP"—a Unique Selling Point. That is, he tries to find something to offer that no competitor offers; something no competitor is *able* to offer. In my own case, I offered more than one USP in my seminar brochure referred to above. I offered a "graduate" program, and I offered to help attendees formulate basic strategies for winning contracts as well as teaching them a number of inside tips.

None of this is to say that I was the only one around who could make these offers, but I was the only seminar producer who made these particular offers. It is reasonable to assume that my seminar was an opportunity to gain unique information!

What matters is not that what you claim is indeed exclusive or unique, but that it is worthwhile as a benefit and that no one else has specifically promised it, so that it *appears* to be exclusive or unique. That makes it a USP. At the same time, it is important to remember that, in being different or novel in some way, you do not lose touch entirely with the familiar. People in general resist change. Somehow, we are all more comfortable with what is known to us by linking what is new with something old and familiar. This is especially important if you are asking your prospects to give up something they are using in favor of your newer methods.

THE UNIQUE SELLING MECHANISM

Once in a while an imaginative marketer comes along with a truly new idea for selling—a "USM" or Unique Selling Mechanism. In its time, each of many common selling mechanisms of today were such USM's. Alfred C. Fuller created such a new idea when he made his door-to-door salesmen dealers—a sales system that is in wide use today by many direct sales manufacturers. Pyramid sales systems, such as that of Amway, among others, were once a radical new idea. Now they represent an accepted mode of direct selling. Essentially, the pyramid is made up of a steadily widening stream of new dealers, since each dealer may recruit his or her own subordinate dealers, to a depth of several levels. Pricing and profit structures are designed to accommodate this, and dealers may rise to higher levels, if they show enough sales success, making room at the bottom of the pyramid for new dealers. (See Figure 10.)

In the same manner, advertising is not always intended to produce sales for products directly, or even sales leads. Some advertising is designed to produce dealers. The multilevel or pyramid-sales companies do much of their recruiting of new dealers by advertisements that invite interested people to mass gatherings, which have the air of a combined seminar and national convention. Already-established dealers are present in abundance to testify to their own prosperity as dealers and to recruit new second- and third-level dealers for whatever product is being sold.

A major speaker's bureau recently developed what appeared to be a completely new idea in selling their own services. Normally, speakers' bureaus act as booking agents, handling all the details and collecting a commission ranging from 25 to 40 percent of the speaker's fee. However, the nature of speaking is such that the lion's share of the demand is for "name" speakers—national celebrities—who can command high fees, sometimes ranging up to fifteen thousand dollars. Nonetheless, this bureau recently offered to enroll less well known speakers in a course of instruction and book them into speaking engagements without charging booking fees until the student is accomplished enough to command fifteen hundred dollars per engagement.

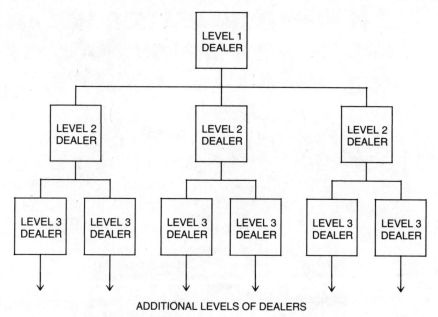

ADDITIONAL LEVELS OF DEALERS

FIGURE 10. Typical pyramid of dealers through several levels.

It was a handsome marketing/sales plan: It provided guaranteed tuition income for the bureau and powerful motivation for the prospect. It does not take high-powered advertising copy to draw customers for this offering. In fact, it was an innovation with antecedents, of course, in the free job-referral service most vocational schools offer their own graduates.

Advertising copy for any such program follows the same guidelines as copy intended to produce sales of products. The chief difference is that in such copy you are not asking for money, except a nominal postage-and-handling sum. Therefore, it should be relatively easy to draw a response without a great deal of text by stressing such factors as "free" and "no obligation." Note, too, that in a great many such advertisements there is the further copy-line notation that "no salesman will call." Furthermore, you must be at great pains in your advertising to instruct the reader exactly what to do. Experience demonstrates the truth of this time and again. For example, Figure 11 is a direct-mail piece sent out by the Massachusetts Department of Commerce Business Service Center to instruct small businesses how to get free services from the state. Note that the message is simple and straightforward. The reader is advised that he need call only one number to get help with business problems. Despite the simplicity of the idea and what the reader is asked to do, there is additional text that spells out in detail what the reader must do to obtain information on the free services offered.

If your business needs assistance from the state, don't call a lot of numbers.

CALL ONE is a toll-free, hassle-free way for business to get the right kind of assistance from the state, right away. Here's how it works.

If your business needs help from the state, CALL ONE: 1-800-632-8181. Tell the person who answers what's on your mind. We'll go to work on your request immediately and get back to you within 5 business days. If some additional time is needed, we'll follow through until you get an answer. It's that simple.

CALL ONE
The one number to call when your business needs assistance from the state.

Massachusetts Department of Commerce Business Service Center
Edward J. King, Governor.   George S. Kariotis, Secretary of Economic Affairs.   James F. Carlin, Commissioner, Dept. of Commerce.

375M-5-80-152749   EST. COST PER COPY $.014

FIGURE 11. Sample direct-mail piece.

THE DIRECT-MAIL PACKAGE

Direct mail is also a form of print advertising. There are several major advantages in using direct mail: It is possible to target prospects precisely, such as physicians, accountants, housewives, etc.; and a single first-class stamp will usually carry approximately five standard-size sheets of paper or their equivalent—room enough for two thousand to three thousand words plus illustrations.

Moreover, the results can be evaluated quickly—sometimes within a few weeks—whereas most media advertising must be booked two to four months in advance. Additionally, tests can be conducted rapidly on a small scale, whereas this is much more difficult to do in print media because of the long lead times required.

Direct mail is especially well suited to the advertiser with a small budget because it is difficult, if not impossible, to do much in media advertising with little money. For example, if your offer requires a full page, you must gamble several thousand dollars for each insertion in any large-circulation publication. Moreover, you will probably be required to pay in advance, so that your money is tied up and not available to you for at least two to three months before you get the service you paid for. This is most difficult for small businesses. In addition to that, if you want to test your offer in several publications to compare results, you will need to lay out quite a large sum of cash.

Direct mail is, therefore, a good solution to the problem, using either rented lists or lists you have built through inquiry advertising and other methods, such as compilation from directories. Here is what the typical mail package contains:

1. A cover/sales letter.
2. A brochure or broadside.
3. An order blank.
4. A return envelope.

In many cases, the package goes well beyond this. It may include several brochures, sometimes samples of some sort, a business card, and, perhaps, a catalog. Some contain special promotional devices, such as a plastic membership card made to resemble a credit card. In other cases, the return envelope is postage paid; some are self-mailers, which require no separate return envelopes.

THE DIRECT MAIL SALES LETTER

For most mail-order specialists, the sales letter is obligatory. Almost anything else may be omitted, but *not* the letter. It falls to the letter to carry the burden of introducing the offer and the reasons for buying to the prospect.

If you have ever gotten one of these direct-mail packages, you may be familiar with the typical letter, as it contains certain distinctive characteristics. If there is a salutation at all, it is "Dear friend." However, there is an increasing trend to do without the salutation and have simply the letterhead with a headline, followed immediately by the text, addressed in the second person to the reader.

The copy is all typed, on a good electric typewriter, except for those relatively few cases of computer-generated letters. It is printed in black or blue ink, with headlines often set off in red ink. Numerous words and phrases may even be underlined or circled with a heavy marking pen for emphasis.

The letter itself explains the basic offer, along with the sales arguments. Sometimes the letters refer to other elements of the package, such as brochures and order forms, but usually the letter is a complete advertisement/solicitation in its own right. Naturally, the letter should follow all the principles of writing advertising sales copy, with the distinct advantage of offering more space for persuasive copy. Therefore, the letter ought to contain an attention-getting, interest-arousing headline, and the text should take up the matter immediately and build interest and buying desire to a peak.

Perhaps marking-pen underlines and circles help, but I have not used them (as you can see in Figure 12), and the letters I have used have pulled adequately for me. I believe that these things are gimmicks, and that they are no substitute for a sound offer that appeals to a legitimate concern. In the case of the letter shown in Figure 12, the motivation was to gain a share—or a larger share—of federal grants and contracts. I posed a rhetorical question which appealed directly to this interest ("Are you getting your share of over $170 billion in federal grants and contracts?"). A boxed paragraph elaborated on the statement of the headline, which, although phrased as a question, flatly stated, "Of course you are not getting your fair share." In case anyone missed the message in the headline, the boxed paragraph served to make it crystal clear.

The body copy established my credentials—the proof that I was qualified and had helped many others. It also made reference to an order form and included several other items, which expanded the sales arguments as well as the proofs.

This package was the result of several years' experience in selling the newsletter, and, although there was nothing basically wrong with my earlier packages as an example of advertising and salesmanship, it did not make the proper offer. It had stressed that the information that would be in the newsletter every month and tried to sell the product rather than what the product would *do* for the buyer. I had wrongly

Government Marketing News
Source Data for
Grants & Contracts

ARE YOU GETTING YOUR SHARE OF OVER $170 BILLION IN FEDERAL GRANTS AND CONTRACTS?

FEWER THAN 2 OUT OF EVERY 100 OF AMERICA'S 13 MILLION BUSINESS AND NON-PROFIT ORGANIZATIONS ARE WINNING A FAIR SHARE OF THE ENORMOUS FEDERAL PROCUREMENT AND GRANTS BUDGETS. AND EVEN AMONG THAT RELATIVE HANDFUL OF ORGANIZATIONS, AN EVEN MORE SELECT GROUP IS GETTING THE LION'S SHARE OF THE MONEY. WANT TO CHANGE THAT? GET SOME--OR MORE--OF IT FOR YOUR OWN ORGANIZATION? HERE'S HOW.

Government Marketing News (a monthly newsletter) and the special publications which back it up are unique. They are a continuous font of grant and contract-winning know-how: news, tips, leads, ideas, techniques to help you win and hold your proper position in the federal marketplace.

I am proud to be the publisher of this information. It enables me to reach an even wider audience than I do with my seminars, lectures, and books. Let me tell you a bit about myself, and please forgive the immodesty--not bragging; just reporting:

I am the author of six books about government marketing, three of which we publish and which are listed in this literature. The others are listed here, too, along with two more I am working on. I have been an aerospace engineer, also worked extensively in technical and general writing, training, safety, energy, and other fields. I have been directly employed by or a consultant to RCA, IBM, Sperry-Rand, GE, Vitro Labs, Chrysler Corporation, World Wide Wilcox, Dun & Bradstreet, the Northeast-Midwest Congressional Coalition, and many other firms. I have been an engineer, technical writer, editorial director, marketing director, and general manager for some of these firms. I have written winning proposals to the U.S.Forest Service, U.S.Navy, U.S. Army, OSHA, FAA, EPA, DOT, GSA, USPS, OEO, OE, Civil Service Commission, India, Greece, Jordan, and the Sudan. I have also been a government employee and a consultant to government agencies. My seminars have been attended by Bethlehem Steel, Control Data Corporation, Genasys, Sikorski Aircraft, Hamilton Standard, Calspan, Boeing Computer Services, Western Union, Vitro Labs, U.S.Industries, Alcoa, Computer Sciences Corporation, and several other major corporations, as well as many small companies. And here are some of those "other" books I mentioned:

Government Contracts: Proposalmanship and Winning Strategies, Plenum Publishing Corporation, New York, 1979.
The $100 Billion Market: How to do Business With the U.S. Government, AMACOM (American Management Associations), New York, 1980.
How to Write the Winning Proposal, McGraw-Hill, New York, scheduled for 1981.

(Two more contracted for, scheduled for 1981 publication.)

Obviously, a single idea or tip which helps you win a single grant or contract is worth many times the modest subscription price, not so? That is, can you afford not to have this marketing information on your desk every month?

An order form is enclosed. Just give us a fast reaction, and I promise you an equally fast fulfillment of your order--by return mail.

Government Marketing News
Box 6067   Wheaton, MD 20906

Cordially,

Herman Holtz
Editor/Publisher

FIGURE 12. A typical sales letter in a direct mail package.

assumed that readers, because they were all successful business people, could make the transition from the promise to provide good information on what was going on in the federal grant and contract markets to winning more grants and contracts. Vain hope! Even sophisticated executives of large companies did not make that connection, and the earlier newsletter languished until I realized that I was testing language and packaging instead of the basic concept of the offer itself.

A small sample (three hundred pieces) tested the idea of selling help in winning contracts per the letter shown in the example and produced excellent results. Suddenly, the largest companies were becoming subscribers, whereas almost all of the earlier subscribers had been small companies and self-employed individuals. Thus, continuous testing, with a variety of changes, has satisfied me that while there are many factors influencing results, the major ones are only two: *the offer itself and the clarity of explanation.*

In sum, your copy must do the following:

1. Make an offer/promise that strikes a nerve and explain it clearly so that it cannot be misunderstood.
2. Prove the offer/promise is legitimate and valid.
3. Tell the prospect exactly what to do next.

11

How to Get Free Advertising

Ironically, free advertising is far more effective than paid advertising and has often created successful enterprises almost overnight.

WHAT IS FREE ADVERTISING?

One very successful entrepreneur, Joe Cossman, advocates in his seminars that the entrepreneur spend not one cent for paid advertising before exploring, utilizing, and exhausting all opportunities for free advertising. He is an expert at the art of getting free advertising and has made profitable use of it.

What most people refer to when they speak of free advertising is public relations or publicity. It includes getting your name and whatever you sell publicized in the media—newspapers, magazines, radio, and TV. There are many ways to do it and individuals and companies who are expert at this sell their professional services to others who need or want publicity. You can retain a public relations firm and pay them to get you publicity, which makes it not free any more.

However, you can do a great deal of this on your own behalf, as many other small entrepreneurs do. Of course, some costs are involved for even the basic PR activity, but the costs are generally modest, and publicity has the enormous advantage of eliminating the skepticism factor of paid advertising.

For example, when *Time* magazine ran a story on Gary Dahl's Pet Rock idea when no one had yet heard of the item, the publicity was worth far more than its equivalent in purchased space. In fact, the item was an overnight sensation, a fad that peaked and declined rapidly, although it afforded its creator the opportunity to become quite wealthy. It is most doubtful that a million dollars' worth of paid advertising would have had the same effect.

THE NEWS RELEASE

The most common and most widely used—and misused—tool of publicity is the news release or press release. The daily flood of news releases into the city room of any newspaper is enormous. A lot wind up in wastepaper baskets, but an equal amount are worthwhile products for many who are able to write news releases that editors will find useful. Generally, editors will publish information contained in news releases when the release is truly deemed newsworthy. That is the secret of developing and profiting from news releases: to make them be perceived as newsworthy.

Essentially, a news release is written around a single story. Its form may vary, but typically it has a letterhead first page which announces it as a news release, press release, or simply a release. It may carry a release date, especially if it is sent out ahead of the event it announces and the preparer wishes the information held for publication until that date arrives. The head data should include a telephone number to call for details.

More important, for your purposes, is what goes into the body of the release. The writer of the release will prepare it in a news or feature style, double-spaced, in the expectation that the editor will use it as written, but rarely does this happen. Occasionally, the editor may assign someone to call the contact indicated on the release to get more information, but it is far more likely that the editor will assign the piece some specific amount of space and cut the story to fit. Hence, the need for double spacing.

You may be struck by the similarity between the news release and the sales letter: Both have headlines and neither is addressed to anyone in particular. For such agencies as the U. S. Labor Department, that's pure coincidence. A newspaper story needs a headline or, at least, a caption of some sort. For every other entrepreneur who is trying to achieve free advertising by using news releases, it's not coincidence: The news release *is* a sales letter.

THE NEWS RELEASE
AS A SALES LETTER

In Hollywood fiction, publicity consists of organizing a spectacular event that causes reporters to fight for the right to report it on the front pages of their papers. In life, that is the exception rather than the rule. It's a struggle to persuade editors to use 10 percent of what you release as news; therefore, if you are to succeed in winning some free publicity via the news release, you must make the release sell itself. That is, you must

News Release

GSA Awards $106 Million in Contracts for 19,000 Vehicles During August

The General Services Administration awarded more than $106 million in contracts for 19,202 vehicles during August.

The largest contract, to the AM General Corp., was for 18,132 mail delivery trucks, costing $100,124,904. The small trucks, which will have right hand steering and a gasoline engine, will be produced in South Bend, Ind., and delivered to the govenment at the rate of 800 a month over the next two years.

Other major awards were made to the Chrysler Corp. for 989 K cars and 34 light trucks. These vehicles, valued at $5,548,601, will be produced at Chrysler assembly plants in Warren, Mich.; Windsor, Ontario; Newark, Del.; and Detroit, Mich., and delivered over the next four months.

The AM General Corp. received an additional contract for $409,434 to produce 47 light fourwheel drive trucks at its Toledo, Ohio assembly plant.

\#   \#   \#

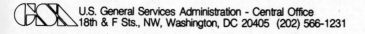

U.S. General Services Administration - Central Office
18th & F Sts., NW, Washington, DC 20405 (202) 566-1231

FIGURE 13. A typical news release.

regard the editor as a customer/prospect, and motivate the editor to use your copy by providing good reasons to do so.

If you examine the content of your daily newspaper, you will see three basic kinds of material used: straight news stories, feature stories, and special features. The latter are primarily things bought from syndicates—columns, puzzles, comic strips, and other such material. Feature stories fall somewhere between hard news and special features, and include such things as human-interest stories and "side-bar" stories, which relate directly to some major news story; for example, the background or brief biography of a recently elected official. However, there is one more category: fillers. These are the little items used to fill chinks in the columns. Like plaster, they are crafted to fill whatever number of lines are blank and bear such news as "The blue whale is the largest mammal on earth," or "The movie industry uses up nineteen billion feet of acetate each year."

Some of the characteristics that will make your release worthy of publication are:

1. The information is novel.
2. The item consists of startling, "believe it or not" kind of information.
3. It is amusing.
4. It happens to shed interesting light on something currently in the news.
5. It's of special interest to the readers of a particular publication.

With a little research, you can almost always dig up something novel, interesting, startling, unusual, or otherwise intriguing—and related to whatever you sell. In my own case—selling information about government grants and contracts, and how to win them—it was easy because the government does so many unbelievable and even irrational things. Among the many things I could use to write news releases around was the sheer dollar size of the federal market (over $100 billion annually), some of the novel procurement contracts (for go-go dancing, renting mules, scattering sterilized flies from the air), and the size of the establishment (over 130,000 people in purchasing functions alone). The same sort of digging can be done for even the most prosaic enterprise. You can develop interesting information for releases by looking in the public library for the history of your product or service. How old is it? Where and how did it start? How did ancient civilizations use it? Answer such questions as: How is what you sell handled in other countries? Especially, how is it done in exotic countries in which the people are quite different from your own? What's the future for what you sell? Have experts made predictions? Can you make a few? What city/state/country/civilization makes the greatest use of what you sell? Why? Who makes the least use of it? Why?

**Coalition
for
Common
Sense
in
Government
Procurement**

1990 M Street, N.W. Suite 570
Washington, D.C. 20036
(202) 331-0975

NEWS RELEASE

September 30, 1981

Contact: Gloria Gamble
(202) 331-0975

COALITION HOSTS 1981 FALL PROCUREMENT CONFERENCE

WASHINGTON, D.C. -- The COALITION FOR COMMON SENSE IN GOVERNMENT PROCUREMENT will host its 1981 Fall Procurement Conference on November 4, 1981. This fall's conference topics will focus on "The New Administration's Commercial Product Policies."

Key agency procurement officials have been invited to be guest speakers. They include:

- GSA Administrator Gerald Carmen

- GSA's new Associate Administrator for Operations Steven Hammer

- GSA's new Associate Administrator for Policy and Management Systems Charles (Terry) Davis

- DOD's new Deputy Undersecretary for Acquisition Management William Long

- OFPP Administrator Donald Sowle

- GSA/FSS Furniture Center Director Peter Boulay

- SBA's Associate Administrator for Procurement Assistance Robert McDermott

FIGURE 14. Another example of a news release.

If you start chasing after the answers to such questions, take a large notebook with you as you'll soon come across literally hundreds of ideas in one afternoon.

MAKING NEWS

You don't have to be the House of Representatives or the Senate to make news. You can create news events. A contest is good for several releases as it progresses, and lends itself to ample photo opportunities, which is always good publicity. To be valid, it doesn't have to be a major undertaking. For example, if you sell a packaged product, slip some kind of token in a few of your fulfillments to announce prizes to be awarded. On the other hand, if you have a retail establishment, you might revive the ancient guess-how-many-beans-are-in-the-jar contest or some derivative thereof. Even staging a contest for the most unusual costume or disguise is excellent publicity—you may attract local papers to cover the event.

Few publicity seekers send something more than a printed release, so sending a full press kit, including a few photographs, makes for a livelier presentation. Those with products to sell, especially products that can be illustrated, ought to send photos to the new-products departments of magazines and newspapers to enhance the chances for publication. For example, the first sample news release shown (Figure 13) might have included a photo of one of the vehicles contracted for. A good photo that is relevant to the story will multiply the probability that the release will be used, because all editors like photos and often use a story they would not otherwise use if it comes with good photos.

DON'T CONFINE YOURSELF TO NEWSPAPERS

News releases are not written for newspapers alone. Send your news releases to magazines, newsletter publishers, the newsrooms of radio and TV stations, and anywhere else you think a placement is possible. However, it you want to increase the probability of your item being used, address it to a specific individual within each medium. That is, when you send your release to the Millersville *Daily Blade*, you are relying on whomever opens your envelope to forward it to the proper party. It is likely to wind up in the wastebasket this way. Every news organization and most publications are organized into departments, and it's worth the time to determine at least which department ought to receive your release.

OTHER PUBLICITY MECHANISMS

Many magazines maintain new-product columns and will publish a photo and some text about your product. They prefer to receive black-and-white glossy prints, 8 by 10 inches, but most will accept 4-by-5's which are more convenient to mail and less expensive to prepare.

You can state specifically what the price of the product or service is and how to order it. The publication's readers want this information, and the editor is well aware of that. In fact, editors recognize that most news releases from commercial establishments are sent in pursuit of free advertising, so there is no need to be coy about how commercial your message is, as long as you have given the editor something worth publishing.

The same considerations apply to radio and TV stations. There are numerous local programs seeking interesting guests for interviews. Make your contacts by calling to determine who the producer is of each show that interests you, and make your appeal just as you must do when writing a release—give the producer a *reason* to become interested.

For many enterprises, good publicity can be obtained by being a guest speaker at meetings and conventions or as a guest columnist for newsletters and journals. Of course, not all public appearances produce business, nor does every complimentary article, but they do make an indirect contribution, especially if you are in the kind of enterprise where contacts are important. You will be well served to be a joiner and participant in as many activities as possible, for it is from these exposures that you gain contacts—an integral part of your publicity campaign.

It's a good idea to attend as many conventions, conferences, trade shows, and fairs as possible. Get acquainted with others in your field and in related fields. Sometimes a chance acquaintanceship with a competitor results in new business. Remember, not all contacts have to be potential customers to be useful.

As you make these contacts and widen your circle of acquaintances, let it be known that you are available as a speaker, committee member, and writer. Becoming acquainted with a great many people is something like selling door-to-door: You never know which house will produce the sale, and the one that does is often the one you thought least likely to do so.

Earlier, reference was made to services that offer to produce sales leads at a fixed fee per inquiry. For example, *Parade* magazine, the nationally distributed Sunday supplement, runs such an inquiry promotion periodically, providing a brief descriptive paragraph for fifty or more items. The cost per inquiry is modest compared to paid advertising space, but the circulation of the supplement is so great that it is not unusual for a small paragraph to draw as many as three thousand inquiries for a nominal fee (charge per actual inquiry received).

Another arrangement is referred to as "PO"—per order—advertising. In this, an advertisement asks for the order, with the order and the money coming into the publisher, who retains part of the funds to pay for the ad and forwards the rest to you to fulfill the order. This is called drop shipping, as is any sale in which someone other than the party taking the order does the actual shipping. Under the PO, drop-shipping arrangement, the money is divided according to whatever arrangement you made with the publisher. Frequently, this is a fifty-fifty arrangement. Such deal percentages may vary from forty to sixty-five percent for the advertiser.

Obviously, the item you sell must be such that you can realize a satisfactory profit at fifty percent or less of the retail price. However, if you are handling merchandise which you can mark up at least three times its cost (still a bit thin), you may wish to consider PO sales. In return for a reduced margin of profit, you have free advertising in a no-risk publicity program.

Many major magazines will accept PO programs, although few will admit they accept them. Of course, the reason is they prefer to sell advertising space and they are not fond of risk taking. Nevertheless, on those occasions when they have failed to sell all the available advertising space, there is a good chance they will accept a PO proposal. Keep in mind this may mean that the publication will not guarantee your copy in any given issue, but will run it when unsold space justifies it.

The way to find out about whether a given publication accepts PO advertising is to study the publication. It's easy to spot a PO advertisement: It's one in which the publication lists its own address as the place to send orders. Obversely, if the advertisement lists the publisher's address as the place to mail inquiries, it's a PI (per inquiry) advertisement.

Swapping is yet another way of doing business. A number of small mail-order dealers who can write with reasonable facility have long exchanged their writing labor for free advertising space. The most likely place with which to arrange such swaps are the large number of advertiser publications. The principal content of these publications is advertising, and readers subscribe to them primarily to read the advertisements. The publishers try to incorporate some editorial content and, consequently, most will exchange advertising space for columns written by practicing business people. Many who write these columns in exchange for advertising also syndicate their columns. That is, the writer retains the copyright and does not give any publisher exclusive rights to publication, but supplies the same column each month to a number of these publications. So a single column each month may bring a dozen free advertisements.

Newsletter publishers will often provide free coverage—editorial notices that constitute free advertising. Naturally, the notice must be something relevant to the readership of the newsletter. For example, because such a large percentage of computer software companies pursue government business, I had no difficulty getting free publicity for my proposal-writing offer in newsletters addressed to computer software people. In the same way, once you have become known to newsletter publishers, a brief note or a copy of your sales letter is sufficient to get you coverage without resorting to a formal news release.

A few newsletters accept paid advertising; they are good prospects for PI and PO advertising as well.

DISTRIBUTING NEWS RELEASES

Obviously, you can print and mail your news releases as you print and mail any material. Of course, it is necessary to compile a mailing list of publications and departments within publishing organizations, radio and TV stations who may use your material. However, there are other ways that are less expensive and time-consuming than mailing releases. For example, there is a Washington, D.C., organization (listed in the Appendix) that offers, for a small fee, to distribute four hundred copies of a news release that you supply. Sometimes you can arrange to leave quantities of releases in places where a number of people will pick them up. If attending a convention or trade show, you can often arrange to make your literature, or at least a news release, available to attendees. Moreover, most seminars and lectures include a literature table, with an open invitation to leave business cards, releases, brochures, and other literature.

YOUR OWN NEWSLETTER

A most effective and low-cost marketing tool which is useful for many enterprises is the promotional newsletter. This is used successfully for promoting almost any kind of enterprise, although obviously some enterprises lend themselves better to its use than others.

Developing a newsletter is quite easy. First of all, it need not be of great size. Four pages is quite adequate, although you may wish to make it longer. Nor is it necessary to publish frequently: A quarterly newsletter does nicely and presents no great burden. Moreover, a quarterly newsletter affords you great flexibility in scheduling and establishing deadlines. For instance, your summer edition (the four editions could be named for the seasons) can be issued almost anywhere between May 1 and August 30, according to when is most convenient for you.

There are numerous advantages to newsletter publishing. You don't have to mail all the issues at once, but can mail throughout the quarter, as you build your mailing lists. You don't have to accomplish your entire distribution by mail. Use the newsletter as you do other literature—make it available at suitable events or provide it to other newsletter publishers gratis, with the invitation to quote from it, as long as they credit the source.

If you wish, you can use one of your letterheads as the front page and masthead. However, somewhere along the top of the first page, identify it as a newsletter. The copy itself can be typed on any good typewriter. In fact, many believe that a newsletter ought to be typed to give it an air of spontaneity and up-to-the-minute coverage. The content will not really be news, but it ought to be interesting enough to persuade the recipient to want it and to keep it. Try to insert information that will inspire the recipient to hang on to it by including a calendar of coming events, recipes, or other such items. Finally, be certain you carry some appropriate advertising in it, as that is its main purpose.

The newsletter starts out without charge. Some entrepreneurs later impose a nominal charge, if they reach a point where they believe that it is justified and will produce paid subscriptions. The charge should be enough to cover postage, printing, and mailing.

SOME MISCELLANEOUS CONSIDERATIONS

Bear in mind, when you pursue free advertising or publicity, that you are competing for attention and coverage just as you compete for sales. The editor who must approve your offering is bombarded by similar requests from a great many sources, and it is simply not possible to accommodate everyone, even if all offerings were worthy. Make your own offering different and attractive—creative imagination helps, just as it does in marketing. If you want to maximize the probability of getting publicity, make your releases valuable, amusing, informative, and helpful. In any case, make your releases look professional. Here's a list of important considerations:

1. Do give a release date or indicate "For immediate release."
2. Do provide a contact name, telephone number, and address.
3. Do provide a dateline (city, state, and date of origin).
4. Do double-space your copy.
5. Do indicate at the bottom of the page whether there is more to the story or that this is the end of the story.
6. Do give your writing a businesslike, factual tone.

7. Do write concisely: Give only the facts, then stop.
8. Do minimize the use of adjectives and adverbs in your body copy.
9. Do *quantify* your facts wherever possible.
10. Do search out attention-getting, interest-arousing leads.

12

How to Get Distribution

*For many enterprises, distribution is itself the
main key to or reason for success.*

WHAT IS DISTRIBUTION?

In many quarters, the term *distribution* is synonymous with *marketing*.
Both terms refer to placing the product or service in the hands of the
consumer. In a great many cases, the principal marketing problem is one
of distribution, and the marketing/sales strategy in these cases is primarily one of making the product readily available to the maximum number
of prospective buyers. For example, selling small items, such as candy
bars and magazines, depends on offering these items in thousands of
retail outlets with prominent displays. In many cases, no amount of sales
effort will suffice to make the business profitable if the product is not
widely enough distributed; and in many cases little or no sales effort is
required if the distribution is effective. Thus good distribution equals
good marketing.

WHEN IS DISTRIBUTION A
POSITIVE FACTOR IN SALES
SUCCESS?

Some businesses, as noted, depend on distribution for success, while
other businesses can survive and prosper without wide distribution. For
example, it is quite difficult to succeed in publishing without wide
distribution. This is one reason why many small publications, such as
newsletters and confidential reports, are sold at high prices, as it is
nearly impossible to do otherwise given their limited circulation. On the

other hand, a one-hundred-page magazine with expensive color reproductions can be sold profitably for a dollar or two a copy. The large print order and, especially, advertising revenue made possible by wide distribution makes this possible. Therefore, it is largely the nature of the product that dictates whether it is essential to arrange for wide distribution.

Retailing is another situation entirely, and as a retail outlet, you may depend on limited distribution. If you handle a variety of small-tag items, such as magazines and candy bars, you will not be as dependent on wide distribution. The distinction is that in retail operations it is not *necessary* to survival to achieve widespread distribution. In fact, there have been entrepreneurs (department stores, for example) who have built large fortunes from the proceeds of a single retail outlet.

Naturally, there are enterprises to which it is impossible to apply the distribution factor. Personal and professional services, which depend for their success on the personal skills of the practitioner, appear to be quite difficult to expand beyond a single location or geographic area. Even this is not an unvarying truth; entrepreneurs have been most imaginative in creating expansion methods that involve increased distribution. Franchising is one of the methods most often used, such as the franchising concept applied to the practice of law and dentistry. The number and types of enterprises which do not lend themselves to expansion through wider distribution appear to be shrinking steadily. Perhaps there are virtually no enterprises which cannot be expanded, if entrepreneurs truly wish to do so.

Some of the traditional methods for distributing goods was covered briefly in Chapter 4. Theoretically, the producing organization could build its own chain or network of distribution. However, in practice it usually proves advantageous to distribute through existing organizations whose main purpose is to distribute products. Therefore, in almost all cases, a product goes from its original production or importing source to a distributing organization. The simple fact is that in a great many cases, these established chains are so effective that persuading them to distribute your product(s) almost guarantees success.

Major distributing organizations, with their own interests to protect, evaluate the distribution value of your product before taking it on. For example, your product may compete with a product they already handle. That can constitute cause for refusing to distribute you. Thus, you may have to search for a distributor who will handle your particular product, which may mean that you have to sign up with a distributor who is not one of the leaders in the field.

There are other considerations. A distributor wants some assurance that you are a stable and dependable producer, and they want some kind of marketing backup, such as guaranteed advertising or advertising allowances. This can take the form of cash sums based on sales volume achieved by the distributor, or advertising that the distributor runs which you agree to have billed to you for payment. Some products require that you supply the distributor with point-of-sale marketing tools in the form of banners, streamers, display stands, and other items that help promote sales.

Some distributors may want you to agree that they will be the sole distributors for your product(s) for the areas they serve. You'll have to judge whether it is in your interest to agree to that. However, you can probably write into the distribution agreement certain escape clauses to protect yourself, such as a proviso that exclusive distribution rights are guaranteed to the distributor only on condition that the distributor guarantees you some minimum sales volume.

It may well be that as a small business you are not yet ready to undertake wide distribution—at least not on any kind of guaranteed basis with a major distributing organization. For one thing, it may require far more capital than you can manage, or it may simply be far too sudden a leap for your business. Therefore, you must look to alternatives.

BEING YOUR OWN DISTRIBUTOR

In a number of cases, a primary source acts as the distributing organization. For example, there are a number of major printing establishments that appoint dealers throughout the United States. They equip each with a sales kit and price list and some general instructions about selling their line. The dealer is a free agent and he may even be a printing broker who represents a number of other printing establishments. The effectiveness of the company's distribution is chiefly a factor of how successful they are at recruiting dealers who produce a satisfactory volume of sales.

Figure 15 is part of a sales package sent out by mail, seeking dealers for a line of business manuals. The copy explains itself quite well. It explains to the reader just what the writer, Banet Zlachevsky of Vector Press, offers, and what the reader must do to get started as a dealer for Vector Press publications.

Another way Zlachevsky recruits dealers is through space advertising, as illustrated in Figure 16. His inquiry advertising does not ask for money, but for a self-addressed, stamped envelope. Moreover, if you subscribe to certain publications directed at independent dealers and small entrepreneurs, such as *Specialty Salesman,* you'll find a number of prime sources seeking dealers, brokers, franchisees, manufacturer's representatives, and others who can distribute the advertiser's product(s). The appeals range from small classified advertisements to full-

DEALER'S INFORMATION

Your Vector Press dealership is ABSOLUTELY FREE! Unlike other dealerships, you don't have to pay us anything at all "up-front" as dealer's fee, registration, good-faith deposit, or whatever else. And you don't have to buy circulars or anything else from us either. Just paste down your own name and address on top of ours in the enclosed order-getting circulars, and take them to any printer as camera-ready copy.

We dropship under your own name. Just send us your mailing labels with each client's name and address, and the books to be dropshipped to that particular client typed or printed clearly on the label's back (gummed) side, enclose the corresponding payment -- and that's all there is to it! For BIGGER PROFITS stock up the fast-selling Vector Press books at out low wholesale prices and fill the orders yourself. New dealers: To get immediate shipment of orders within 24 hours from our receipt of your order please send us cash, money order, or certified check (personal checks take over 2 weeks to clear).

And that's not all. When you insert your ads through our own Advertising Agency, without any extra costs or charges at all we will provide you with highly-appealing copy for your ads plus FREE PROFESSIONAL COUNSELING AND ADVICE to help you sell more -- since the more Vector Press books you sell the more that we will all profit.

Use the handy form below to order now sample copies of these fast-moving publications, without any risk on your part thanks to our FULL MONEY BACK GUARANTEE, and see for yourself how you can easily rake-in the profits!

------------------------Cut out and send your order TODAY!----------------------

Rush to me postpaid by 3rd or 4th class mail the following publications.

Quantity @ Each Total

[] "FREE SOURCES & HANDOUTS" Manual . . . . _____ $_____ $_____

[] HOW TO MAKE BIG PROFITS SELLING BOOKS BY MAIL. . . _____ $_____ $_____

[] "SHOESTRING BUSINESS" Manual - Volume 1. . . . . . _____ $_____ $_____
                                 Volume 2. . . . . . _____ $_____ $_____
                                 Volumes 1 and 2 . . _____ $_____ $_____

[] SAVE $3.00! Sample set of all three Manuals above
               for only $12.00 per each set. . . . . _____ $_____ $_____

[] INTERVIEWING FOR SURVEYS & POLLS (4 volumes) . . . _____ $_____ $_____

[] SAVE $10.00! Complete sample set of all four pub-
                lications above for only $24.95/set . _____ $_____ $_____

[] Postage & handling for AIR MAIL or to overseas by BOAT for samples or dropshipping. Each Manual: USA & Canada by AIR MAIL $1.50. Overseas $1.00 by BOAT or $3.00 by AIR MAIL. All 3 Manuals: USA & Canada by AIR MAIL $3.00. Overseas $2.00 by BOAT or $6.00 by AIR MAIL. Interviewing Course: USA & Canada by AIR MAIL $3.00. Overseas $3.00 by BOAT or $9.00 by AIR MAIL. All 4 Publications: USA & Canada by AIR MAIL $4.50. Overseas $4.00 by BOAT or $14.00 AIR MAIL. (WHOLESALE: Indicate quantities and type of shipment by boat or by air mail and we will quote the total shipping costs.) . $_____

NAME _____

ADDRESS _____

California residents only, please add the 6% Sales Tax (if for resale, send only the Seller's Permit number instead of the Tax). . . . $_____

Total remittance enclosed in [] cash, [] check, or [] money order. . . . . . $_____

CITY, STATE, & ZIP CODE _____

Vector Press P.O.Box 4451, 66 Ocean View Ave., Santa Barbara, Calif. 93103

FIGURE 15. Typical dealer recruiting literature. *(Courtesy Vector Press, Box 4451-H, Santa Barbara, CA 93103.)*

page and double-page spreads. Here is a list of a few of the products and services for which dealers are being sought.

Costume jewelry, to be sold on the "party plan."

Sealers and related products for roofing, siding, parking lots.

Health food area managers, if your initial order is big enough, and for which you get exclusive rights in five or ten counties.

Gift items, to be sold by mail, using supplied catalogs.

Novelties and costume jewelry, on cards, to be sold to retail outlets.

Badges and photo buttons, with equipment for their manufacture.

Carpet and furniture cleaning, service business, with equipment you buy.

Shoes, sold from catalog, with samples.

Porcelain repair dealer-service.

Bumper stickers for which, like badges, you buy equipment and manufacture.

Success-motivation cassette tapes to place in retail establishments.

Greeting cards, building a route of retail outlets that you service regularly.

Outdoor signs, order taking.

MAKE REAL MONEY!

Sell Anything Fast With Our Order - Getting Ads, Sales Letters, Circulars, Catalogs, News Releases . . .

ON JUST A SHOESTRING BUDGET!

We Provide Advice, Guidance, "Angles", Money-Making Ideas . . . to:

- Start or Expand Your Own Business on a shoestring and develop your own products, services, and ideas.
- Become a Drop-Shipper/Wholesaler and let others do all the work, advertising, and selling for you.
- Publish and sell on a Shoestring your own books, folios, manuals, guides, courses, newsletters . . . that we research and ghostwrite to sell fast.
- Free Professional Counseling without obligation: Tell us what you want to accomplish or send us your sales materials. We'll show you how to get started, increase sales, make more money!

FOR INFORMATION, SEND SELF-ADDRESSED ENVELOPE, TWO STAMPS.

BANET ZLACHEVSKY MARKETING RESEARCH

Box 4451-B-59, Santa Barbara, Calif. 93103

FIGURE 16. Example of inquiry advertising paid for by written column. *(Courtesy Vector Press, Box 4451-H, Santa Barbara, CA 93103.)*

As you can see from this small sampling, virtually everything is sold via dealers and brokers or representatives. Since most of those advertisements run month after month, I am compelled to conclude that they are successful and attract enough responses to make the advertising expenditure worthwhile.

Another vehicle many use to recruit dealers and representatives, as well as to make direct sales, is the bound volume of advertising postcards. Although the publishers of these items also sell straight advertising display space, the primary strategy is to print postcard-sized advertisements, with the copy and a block to record one's name and address on one side, while the other side is a self-addressed postcard. It could hardly be easier to make inquiry. Those who produce these items mail them by the thousands, and since a great many of the advertisers keep their advertisements running steadily in these publications, it must be presumed that they receive a satisfying number of cards returned in the mail regularly.

Recruiting dealers and representatives in this manner has its problems. The vast majority of dealers who sign up fail to produce enough sales to make the dealership worthwhile to either party. It exhibits the same characteristics that any sales effort does: Some small percentages of the prospects actually become paying customers. When you sign up dealers, a similarly small percentage become worthwhile dealers. Not surprisingly, the easier you make it for individuals to sign up as dealers, the more you will sign up. Therefore, you must decide what your policies and practices will be in recruiting dealers.

FULFILLMENT CONSIDERATIONS

There are two basic ways in which you can fulfill orders: They can be filled by drop shipment, wherein you fill the orders for the dealers, or the dealer can carry the merchandise and do the fulfillment directly. Of course, there are some circumstances in which the fulfillment method is dictated by the product. Printing, for example, can only be handled by drop shipment, since each order is a custom order. Then again, there may be cases where the product is so costly that it is difficult to find dealers who can afford to carry an inventory. On the other hand, there are some types of merchandise for which the customer will not agree to wait for future delivery but expects to consummate the sale on the spot. This all but mandates that the dealer carry a stock of merchandise.

Most importantly, everyone who deals by mail soon learns that the world is full of curiosity seekers and daydreamers who will send off for anything offered without obligation, but will never make the final decision to act decisively. Offer free dealership and a sales kit, and you'll have many applicants—many new "dealers," in fact, if you accept all applicants without screening in any manner. Those who distribute through dealers generally cope with this in one of two ways:

1. Accept and work with all, even those who produce only an occasional sale and never work seriously at being dealers.
2. Screen applicants in some manner, rejecting those who are obviously not serious and likely to be wasting your time.

The theory used to justify the first way of handling the problem is that it is worth putting up with all the ineffective dealers and time wasters to find the handful of hardworking, serious dealers who produce results. One small publisher of a newsletter and self-help reports told me, when I questioned him on the subject, that he had fifteen hundred "dealers," of which perhaps ten or fifteen were producing significant results. Since it all added up to a business showing a reasonable profit, he was not inclined to disturb the arrangement. He believed that those dealers who were not producing—hence not making any money for themselves— would automatically drop out. Unfortunately, that's a vain hope: Some do drop out, but many go on wasting your time with correspondence and accounting needs in exchange for an occasional small order on which the profit does not justify the work.

Turning to the second alternative, you will find that there are several ways to reduce the numbers of ineffectual dealers you acquire, if not to eliminate them entirely. There are a number of measures you can take, although the various measures are all designed to qualify the applicants, much as you qualify a sales prospect before you spend a great deal of your time on the sales effort. In the case of the dealer applicant, qualifying means screening out those who are not serious and/or not competent to be effective dealers. One method some entrepreneurs use is simply to require the applicant to buy a starting inventory. Only those who are serious about being dealers will invest their money. Presumably, this also says something for the applicant's capability for being effective as your dealer. You may assume that no one will make an inventory investment without some confidence in his or her ability to make sales.

Some entrepreneurs are indifferent to this, especially those who do not guarantee exclusive sales territories, since they lose absolutely nothing by the transaction, but do gain some merchandise sales. However, if you do tie up territories when you accept dealers, you may wish more assurance that the dealer is a qualified person, and you may ask for references.

In other dealership arrangements, as noted, it is not practical for the dealer to carry inventory, but he or she does need a sample case or some kind of sales kit that is fairly costly. Therefore, the firm charges the dealer a deposit, refundable either upon some volume of sales or upon returning the sales kit in good condition. Again, this screens out those who are not serious about their desire to be dealers. In some arrangements, such as the general plan followed by Fuller Brush Company and Avon, the dealer needs only a sample case and brochures or a catalog, but he is encouraged to stock the fast-moving items so as to be able to make immediate delivery. Extra discounts are allowed to encourage dealers to carry inventory.

FRANCHISING

Franchising is an idea that has gained a great deal of interest in recent decades, and it has been the means for many entrepreneurs to make large fortunes and build businesses more rapidly than they could have done with more traditional methods. The key to success is having other investors take the risk, while granting you a small percentage of their profits. In return, the franchisee gets the benefits of using your established name and reputation and your expert guidance in starting and managing the enterprise.

McDonald's, the most prominent fast-food chain, is also the most successful franchise operation in history. Certainly, it has inspired scores of imitators, and franchising has spread to other kinds of enterprises, such as instant-copy print shops and legal services. However, the basic requirement is that the franchisor has built a successful and well-known enterprise. He must be able to present a franchisee with a specific model and detailed procedural guidance. The name and record of success are especially important to inspire franchisees with enough confidence to invest substantial capital.

DIRECT DISTRIBUTION

The foregoing examples have covered indirect methods of distribution through dealers and franchisees. Many enterprises have been highly successful without using networks of dealers and distributors, through direct-response marketing—selling directly to the consumer. One example of success in direct-response marketing is Chicagoan Ron Popeil. For nine years he sold food-cutting kitchen appliances in a Chicago Woolworth. He was quite successful at it, earning one-thousand-dollars a week. By that time, television had become a well-established medium and that started him wondering what would be the result if he put his demonstration on TV. He had a sixty-second commercial made, took it to another city for a test, and bought some air time. It took only three days for the store to sell out the entire stock! Forming a partnership with a friend, Popeil then took the proposition to other cities and managed to gross nearly a quarter million his first year. It grew to nearly nine-million-dollars a year after five years, at which time he went public. Today, the firm markets a variety of products by direct-response TV advertising. Significantly, Popeil says that the first thing he wants to know when considering a new product is what problem it solves. That is the key to his commercials: He doesn't sell products; he sells solutions to problems.

Today, there are many others who use the same methods. Many TV sales promotions call for orders addressed to the same box number or telephone number on a PO agreement, wherein the station gets some fixed fee for each order taken. A great deal of late-night TV commercials selling gadgets, jewelry, watches, novelties, and other such small items are sold in this way. That's one of the reasons most of these offerings are made on the independent stations—they tend to be the smaller stations with good local coverage.

There is another effective way to reach a mass audience and achieve high-volume sales in direct-response marketing—mail order. This involves two broad methods of attack: reaching prospects by advertising in various publications, and reaching prospects by direct-mail solicitations. Fulfillment is generally by mail, although when the item sold is bulky, some mail-order entrepreneurs prefer to utilize the delivery services of private-sector express companies.

The best-known mail-order companies are probably Sears and Montgomery Ward, both of whom also operate great department store chains. However, there are a many other important mail-order enterprises, not as well known, but quite successful. One of these is Frederick's of Hollywood, which started in New York, using the mails exclusively at first, and only later moving to Hollywood to open a chain of retail outlets. Still, over twenty-five percent of the firm's business is done by mail, achieving over one third of its profits from that sales volume.

This clearly indicates the efficiency of mail and other direct-response marketing. It is ordinarily far less costly to distribute by mail or TV commercial than by operating costly retail stores, paying commissions, or discounting to dealers and jobbers.

The question occurs, if mail order is more profitable than other ways of distributing, why do successful mail-order enterprises open retail outlets? The reason is that there are many customers who do not like to shop by mail. Opening retail outlets probably does create some competition with one's own mail-order marketing, but it also brings in many customers who could not be otherwise won.

The reverse is also true. Many retail operations increase their volume, without adding greatly to their costs, by using the mails to reach out-of-town customers. For example, many camera stores run full-page advertisements in photography magazines, offering their wares by mail. The same is true for a great many other retail businesses. Mail offers expansion without adding to overhead. The sole additional costs are advertising costs.

13

Tying It Together

*Products change, methods change, conditions
change; but the nature of people does not
change, so basic business verities continue to be
true.*

The French say *Plus ça change, plus c'est la même chose*—the more things
change, the more they stay the same—to remind us that while things
appear to change constantly, in some respects the change is superficial.
It's as true in business as it is in other things. With new things to sell, new
ways to make offerings, new ways to achieve distribution, there are still
many verities which do not change, and they may be defied and violated
only at the risk of disaster. It is still true that an enterprise must be built,
and overly rapid expansion is quite dangerous. It is still true that every
enterprise must provide a useful service to its customers if it is to survive
and build a reliable following. It is still true that all marketing depends
on making the customer see clearly what the offered product or service
will *do* for him or her. That is, the customer must be given a *reason* to
buy, and that reason must be something he perceives as a benefit. It is
also essential that the customer *understand* exactly what the benefit is,
and that is where a great deal of marketing falls short.

Here are two examples, illustrating the two extremes:

A four-inch advertisement on an inside page of a current magazine
starts with the following copy:

WE'LL DROP-SHIP YOU TO SUCCESS!
NO INVESTMENT-NO GAMBLE-NO RISK!
NO STOCK TO BUY!
40 BRAND NEW TOWELS $1.75!

There can be no doubt as to what the advertiser is offering or why
he thinks the reader should stop and read. The body copy goes on to

expand on the headlines and provide additional detail and price information.

In the opposite column is another advertisement, headlined:

THE BIG SELLER FOR '81
PRE-ENTRY PROTECTION

After this mysterious headline, the body copy goes on to explain that it is offering a fabulous alarm, suitable for protecting cars and buildings, but it provides no further information except for the price and claims of how lightning-fast sales will be to anyone who deals in this item. There is no additional information on what the item does.

The difference between the two advertisements is that one may assume it is not necessary to provide more information about as common an item as a towel, but the same assumption ought *not* to be made for an alarm of any kind. Even a reader familiar with security devices cannot tell from this advertisement whether the device is sonic, pressure-sensitive, hard-wired, or on what basis it works. Anyone investing money in the device is likely to want to know just what kind of device it is. In all cases, the advertiser must make a sensible judgment as to what a reader *needs to know*.

An editor once admonished me, "It's not enough to write so that you can be understood; you must write so that you *cannot be misunderstood*." In the cases cited, the first advertisement gave the reader a reason to buy: an extraordinarily low price for even the smallest and thinnest of towels. The second advertisement provided absolutely no reason, except a vague claim that it's the "big seller for '81." What should the second advertisement have offered? Whatever feature the alarm had that made it worthy of special attention—wireless, battery-operated from simple flashlight cells, the latest technology, reliability, its small size, and so on.

There is a vast difference between a *claim* and *factual information*. With the right facts, you don't need to make claims; you simply *report*. Say that you've already sold over twenty-two thousand this year, instead of claiming that you're breaking all sales records. Is twenty-two thousand a record-breaking number? Maybe not, but who knows that? It's not likely that the reader will. At least it says *something*, where "breaking all records" says nothing—unless you can prove it.

Selling and advertising are *persuasive* tactics. Few of today's prospects are so naïve or unsophisticated as to be swayed by pure hyperbole. They know that frequently, the greater the claim, the poorer the product. Therefore, it is essential that you not confuse "hype" with logic. Logic doesn't sell anything, but emotional appeals do; and customers must be persuaded to *want* something—the result promised—and then be supplied with the rationale for the decision. The smart marketer makes us want to believe that what he or she is selling will produce the benefit promised. Most importantly, the prospect must be encouraged to believe that his decision is one any reasonable, intelligent adult would make.

Marketing is expensive. The elements of it cost a great deal of money: space for print advertising, radio and TV time, postage and printing for direct mail, sales commissions, and everything else required to reach the market with your offer. Therefore, you can't afford to waste dollars appealing to people who are not prospects for what you have to offer. Don't expect readers of the *National Enquirer* to be the best prospects for stocks and bonds, nor waste your advertising dollars trying to sell frilly underwear to the few women who read men's magazines. You must know exactly to whom your offers are best addressed and getting the answer to that question is very much a part of marketing. It is derived by research, reading relevant trade literature, and by testing.

There is also the matter of doing it the other way around. If you have not yet made the full commitment and still have options as to just *what* you wish to deal in, reversing the usual marketing order means determining what kinds of customers you can reach most effectively, and then deciding what you can offer. For example, you might have access to a line of expensive jewelry at good discounts. If you are at the stage where you are planning to initiate the enterprise, but still have many options open, it is a good first step to draw up a list of the things you can offer and the prospects you can reach. See what the match-ups are. This kind of marketing exercise may surprise you and delight you by producing possibilities which would not otherwise have occurred to you.

Even when marketing an essential item, there are temporary surges in sales as a result of some outside factor, such as a news story in a prominent publication or the introduction of a new, wholly unique product. It's quite important to make sensible judgments as to the normal size of a market and not to be misled into unwise expansions and inventory overstocks by such special situations. Food processors, for example, enjoyed a boom market for some time after they were introduced. Early models were priced high, but a multitude of competing brands were soon introduced into the marketplace. Those who stocked up on the high-priced models soon found themselves running sales to get rid of excess inventory.

A successful enterprise of any kind will soon produce competition in a volume proportionate to its initial success. The initial success tends to be at a high price because the originator generally enjoys an "exclusive" or something close to it. As competition enters the market— and it often materializes sooner than expected—some of the competition will offer lower prices. Therefore, if you are one of those early in the market, expect competition at competing prices. If you have captured a good share of the market, be prepared to defend your turf to keep your share of the market.

On the other hand, rarely does a product or service meet with instantaneous success without heavy marketing effort. Those who sell the item must *make* the market—introduce the item, make the public aware of its existence and usefulness, and create the desire to own one. In this sense, competition is to be desired, for no one can make a market alone. The proper objective of marketing is to capture a fair share of the market for yourself.

One of the primary mistakes that costs many entrepreneurs their businesses is losing touch with the market. Despite the quotation that opened this chapter, some things *do* change, and you must adapt to it. You cannot do this unless you detect and recognize that change is occurring and learn precisely what the change is. Trucking companies took the freight business from the railroads, while airlines took over most of their passenger business. Perhaps the railroads would have inevitably declined, but in recent years railroads have done a few things they should have done many years ago, such as piggybacking truck trailers loaded with automobiles on flatcars for cross-country hauling. In general, American industry is suffering from competition, at least partially because Japan and others installed newer and more efficient manufacturing equipment, while American industrialists failed to replace their obsolescent plants.

One way to avoid losing touch with your market is by continual market research. Large corporations have large marketing departments, but small enterprises do not enjoy such luxuries. Nonetheless, there are other ways to reach the same goals.

1. Read the periodicals in your own field to keep up to date.
2. Join the relevant trade associations and professional groups. Participate in trade shows, conventions, and the like.
3. Monitor the results of your marketing continually. Make *every marketing campaign a test*. Study the results, look for changes, and investigate the changes as to *why* sales have increased or declined.
4. React quickly to all changes. Try out new marketing ideas, new promotions, new advertising techniques, new media.
5. Be absolutely ruthless in cutting losses. Don't flog a dead horse. If an item doesn't sell well, despite your best efforts, drop it. Concentrate on what sells. Don't be trapped into spending most of your marketing effort to achieve only 10 percent of your sales. Forget prestige—there's more prestige in earning good profits than in proving that you can make a loser pay its way while you neglect the rest of your business.
6. *Don't confuse selling with marketing.* Selling is only taking orders that marketing has identified. Marketing is almost everything from selecting what is to be sold, to identifying the prospects and how to reach them, to fulfilling orders. These things change, and you must change with them, if you are to remain in business for the long haul.

Appendix:
The Basic Reference File

Marketing is a matter of making decisions, enhanced by inputting an adequate amount of information first. In the preceding pages and chapters you have been exhorted to do many things, such as reading trade periodicals, using direct mail, and joining the right associations. Every marketer ought to have a library; among the items listed here for your reference file will be lists of other things that can be useful.

The lists furnished are starter lists. To the maximum extent possible, this Appendix will suggest sources for additional information. The Yellow Pages of many large-city telephone directories are always good sources for finding advertising agencies and services, mailing-list brokers, professional mailers, and other services.

STATE SMALL-BUSINESS PROGRAMS

Most states have special programs for small businesses, minority-owned businesses in particular. They offer a variety of services to assist small businesses, including help in doing business with the state's own purchasing and procurement offices. Following are the contacts supplied by the various states.

ALABAMA
Clyde Chatman
Office of
State Planning
3734 Atlanta Hwy.
Montgomery 36130
205/832-6400

ALASKA
Donald M. Hoover
Div. of Economic Enterprise
Dept. Commerce & Econ. Develop.
675 7th Ave, Station A
Fairbanks 99701
907/452-8182

ARIZONA
Clint E. Johnson
Ofc. Economic Planning & Develop.
1700 W. Washington, Rm. 400
Phoenix 85007
602/255-5374

ARKANSAS
C. A. Hamilton
Small Business Assistance Div.
Arkansas Dept. Economic
Development
One State Capitol Mall
Little Rock 72201
1-800/482-9659

CALIFORNIA
James H. Exum
1823 14th Street
Sacramento 95814
916/322-5060

COLORADO
Bill Scott
Small Business Assistance Center
University of Colorado
Campus Box 434
Boulder 80309
303/492-8211

CONNECTICUT
Frank Silva
State Office Bldg.
Hartford 06115
203/566-4051

FLORIDA
John Kraft
Ofc. of Business Assistance
Executive Ofc. of the Governor
Tallahassee 32301
904/488-9983

HAWAII
Doreen Shishido
Dept. Planning & Econ. Develop.
250 S. King St.
Honolulu 96813
808/548-4616

ILLINOIS
Sam W. Wright
Small Business Coordinator
Dept. of Admin. Services
Stratton Office Bldg., Rm. 802
Springfield 62707
217/782-2249

INDIANA
Mark Hedegard
Ombudsman Office
503 State Office Bldg.
Indianapolis 46204
317/232-3376

IOWA
Iowa Citizen's Aide Office
State Capital
Des Moines 50319
515/281-3592

KENTUCKY
Small Business Development
Section
Small and Minority Business
Development Div.
Kentucky Dept. of Commerce
Capital Plaza Tower
Frankfort 40601
Floyd Taylor: 502/564-2064
Colin Philips, Patsy Wallace:
502/564-2074

LOUISIANA
Andrew Flores, C.I.D.
Office of Commerce & Industry
P.O. Box 44185
Baton Rouge 70804
504/342-5361
Nadia Goodman: 504/342-5366
Mitchell Albert, Director
Louisiana Office of Minority Bus.
Enterprise
P.O. Box 44185
Baton Rouge 70804

MARYLAND
Norman Holmes
The World Trade Center,
Suite 2223
Baltimore 21202
301/383-7877

MASSACHUSETTS
John Cicarelli
Dept. Commerce & Development
Div. of Small Business Assistance
Boston 02202
617/727-4005
1-800-632-8181

MICHIGAN
Edward Bivins
Purchasing Div., Dept. Mgmt. &
Budget

Mason Bldg., 2nd Floor
Lansing 48909
MINNESOTA
Ms. Dolores (Dee) Kauth
Dept. of Economic Development
480 Cedar St.
St. Paul 55101
612/296-5011
MISSISSIPPI
Buddy Mitcham
Sillers Bldg.
Jackson 38205
601/354-6487
MISSOURI
Thomas A. Monks
Div. Community & Econ.
Development
Jefferson City 65102
314/751-4855
MONTANA
John Lopach, Director
Ofc. Commerce & Small Bus.
Develop.
Governor's Office, Rm. 212
Capitol Station
Helena 59601
406/449-3923
NEW JERSEY
Harry J. Callaghan
N.J. Dept. Labor & Industry
Trenton 08625
609/292-9587
Bette Benedict: 609/984-3416
NEW MEXICO
Miriam McCaffrey
Existing Industry Liaison
Economic Development Div.
Santa Fe 85703
505/825-5571
NEW YORK
Raymond R. Norat, Deputy
Commissioner
Div. of Ombudsmen & Small Bus.
Services
230 Park Ave
New York 10017
212/949-9303
NORTH CAROLINA
Albert H. Calloway, Assist. Dir.
Business Assistance Div.
N. Carolina Dept. Commerce

430 N. Salisbury St.
Raleigh 27611
919/733-7980
OHIO
Gordon N. Waltz, Mgr.
Small Business Assistance Office
Dept. Econ. & Community
Develop.
Columbus 43215
614/466-4945
OKLAHOMA
Paul Cartledge
1515 W. Main
Durant 74701
405/924-5094
OREGON
Allan R. Mann
Small Business Office
Dept. Economic Development
Salem 97310
503/378-1200
PENNSYLVANIA
Ms. Densey Jovonen, Director
Small Business Service Center
South Office Bldg., Rm. G-13
Harrisburg 17120
717/787-3003
RHODE ISLAND
Joseph C. Lombardo
Dept. Economic Development
One Weybosset Hill
Providence 02903
401/277-2601
TENNESSEE
Small Business Information Center
Dept. Economic Development
107 Andrew Jackson State Office
Bldg.
Nashville 37219
615/741-1888
800-342-8470 (in Tennessee)
800-251-8594 (from out of state)
TEXAS
Lists programs, including Small
Business Office, but furnishes no
specific contacts
UTAH
Norman V. Hall
Business Development Coordinator
No. 2 Arrow Press Square, Suite
260

165 South West Temple
Salt Lake City 84101
801/533-5325

VERMONT
Elbert "Al" Moulton
Commissioner of Economic
Development
109 State St.
Montpelier 05602
802/828-3221

WASHINGTON
Douglas Clark
Small Business Office
General Administration Bldg.
Olympia 98504
206/753-5614

WEST VIRGINIA
Ms. Eloise Jack, Director
Small Business Service Unit
Governor's Ofc. Economic Develop.
Bldg. 6, Suite B-564

Capitol Complex
Charleston 25305
304/348-0010

WISCONSIN
Ms. Edith Borden
Small Business Ombudsman
Dept. of Business Development
One Wilson St.
Madison 53702
608/266-9465

John Driscoll, Director
State Bureau of Procurement
One Wilson St.
Madison 53702
608/266-1551

VIRGIN ISLANDS
Ulric F. Benjamin, Director
Small Business Development
Agency
Box 2058
St. Thomas 00801
809/774-1331

FEDERAL SMALL-BUSINESS PROGRAMS

There are far too many federal programs and offices, as well as a large number of federally supported programs, to be completely listed here. However, the following will enable you to find those useful to you.

MINORITY BUSINESS DEVELOPMENT AGENCY (MBDA) is an organization within the U.S. Department of Commerce, dedicated to aiding minority entrepreneurs and those minorities deemed "socially and economically disadvantaged" who wish to initiate an enterprise. MBDA, formerly OMBE (Office of Minority Business Enterprise), supports approximately three hundred nonprofit organizations who are charged with furnishing assistance to minority entrepreneurs. To determine which such organizations are nearest you and most suitable to your needs, you can contact the MBDA, U.S. Department of Commerce, Washington, D.C., 20230, and ask for the information you need. Alternatively, you can seek out the nearest regional office of MBDA, listed in the telephone directories for Atlanta, Chicago, Dallas, New York, San Francisco, and Washington, or you can seek out one of the MBDA district offices, located in most major cities. There are approximately thirty-five such offices.

THE SMALL BUSINESS ADMINISTRATION (SBA) offers programs to help small businesses, especially minority-owned small businesses. The SBA central office is at 1441 L Street, NW, Washington,

D.C. 20416, and like MBDA, the SBA has regional offices and district offices, which can usually be found listed in local telephone directories. The SBA has training and counseling programs, conducts free seminars, offers many free publications and other assistance. It contributes to the support of some of the organizations referred to as supported principally by the MBDA budget.

See the section in this Appendix on Useful Books, some of which list these government offices and government-supported nonprofit organizations. One you will find listed there that covers all of this is the *Directory of Federal Purchasing Offices,* which also offers information on "Where, What, How to Sell to the U.S. Government," as well as a great deal of detailed information on the various special programs of agencies other than the SBA and MBDA. For example, the Department of Defense (DOD) has by far the largest procurement budget in the government and offers the greatest opportunity for marketing by small business. Those markets and the several special small-business programs of the sprawling Defense Department are covered also in the *Directory,* as are many lesser-known government markets. The Library of Congress spends approximately $27 million annually for supplies and services, which is a substantial market for many small businesses.

ADVERTISING

Advertising is a huge industry with many facets, as a few minutes spent looking in the Yellow Pages of any large-city telephone directory will soon reveal. Here are some of the subheads listed there:

Advertising agencies, general
Advertising, aerial
Advertising, classified
Advertising, direct-mail services
Advertising directories, guides
Advertising specialties, novelties
Advertising awards, plaques, trophies
Advertising consultants
Advertising copywriters
Advertising illustrators, photographers

MAILING-LIST BROKERS

DUN'S MARKETING SERVICES (Dun & Bradstreet Inc.)/3 Century Drive/Parsippany, NJ 07054/800-526-0065
ED BURNETT CONSULTANTS INC./2 Park Ave./New York, NY 10016/ 800-223-7777

LIST HORIZONS INC./179 West Washington Blvd./Chicago, IL. 60602/ 800-431-2914

MONEY MARKET DIRECTORIES INC./818 E. High/Charlottesville, VA/800-446-2610

NATIONAL DEMOGRAPHICS LTD./624 Market St./Denver, CO 80202/ 800-525-3533

Mailing lists may be ordered in many different ways. For example, there are lists of senior citizens, buyers of books, architects, veterans, and so forth. Many mailing-list brokers specialize in certain types of lists. For example, Dun's Marketing Services specializes in lists related to business firms and business executives. Many of the list brokers have catalogs describing the various lists they make available, and some can even compile any list you want from banks available in their computers.

ADVERTISING SPECIALTIES

ADVERTISING SPECIALTIES INC./Box 401/Raleigh, MS 39153/800- 647-7065

NEW ENGLAND BUSINESS SERVICES/Hollis St./Groton, MA 01450/ 800-225-9550

NEW YORK ADVERTISING GIVEAWAYS/303 5th Avenue/New York, NY/800-628-5037

CLASSIFIED ADVERTISING

RUSSELL JOHNS ASSOCIATES (for *Money, Venture,* and other magazines)/ Box 1510/Clearwater, FL 33517/800-237-9851

CREDIT CARD PLANS

AMERICAN EXPRESS CO./800-528-4800

CARTE BLANCHE/800-421-0081

DINERS CLUB/800-525-7000

For bank cards—Master Card and VISA—apply to a bank in your own area.

CREDIT INFORMATION

COMMERCIAL CREDIT CO./Baltimore, MD 21202/800-525-3565

TRW BUSINESS CREDIT SERVICES/100 Oceangate/Long Beach, CA 90802/800-526-0677

TRADE PUBLICATIONS

Every trade, industry, business, and professional field has trade publications. There are, for example, periodicals such as the following:

Beer Wholesaler

American Bookseller

Ceramic Industry

Kitchen Business

Apparel Industry Magazine

Candy Marketer

California Builder & Engineer

Parking Magazine

There are thousands of such publications; a large number of them are listed in *Writer's Market,* and more may be found listed in each of several other publications. Getting help in locating the periodicals of interest is quite easy. Stop into your public library and ask the reference desk librarian for help.

Useful Books

Among the many books in my own library which I believe are helpful to every business person concerned with marketing are the following:

BARMASH, ISADORE. *For the Good of the Company.* New York: Grossett & Dunlap, 1976.

BETTGER, FRANK. *How I Raised Myself From Failure to Success in Selling.* Englewood Cliffs, N.J.: Prentice-Hall, 1949.

COSSMAN, JOSEPH E. *How I Made $1,000,000 in Mail Order.* Englewood Cliffs, N.J.: Prentice-Hall, 1963.

DIBLE, DONALD M. *Up Your OWN Organization.* New York: The Entrepreneur Press/Hawthorn Books Inc., 1974.

HOLTZ, HERMAN R. *The $100 Billion Market: How to do Business With the U.S. Government.* New York: AMACOM, 1980.

————. *Profit from Your Money-Making Ideas.* New York: Amacom, 1980.

————. *Directory of Federal Purchasing Offices: Where, What, How to Sell to the U.S. Government.* New York: John Wiley & Sons, 1981.

KONIKOW, ROBERT B. *How to Participate Profitably in Trade Shows.* Chicago: Dartnell Corporation, 1977.

SMITH, CYNTHIA S. *How to Get Big Results From a Small Advertising Budget.* New York: Hawthorn Books Inc., 1973.

Some Newsletters

There are many newsletters—thousands of them—covering every conceivable business and subject. Again, the public library is a good place to go to get more information about these. However, there is a modestly priced directory, *The Newsletter Yearbook Directory*, published periodically, which lists a great many newsletters that might be of particular interest to you. The publisher of this directory is:

Howard Penn Hudson
The Newsletter Clearinghouse
44 West Market Street
Rhinebeck, NY 12572
914/876-2081

Some newsletters I have found to be particularly useful are these:

Boardroom Reports, 500 5th Avenue, New York, NY 10036.

Brainstorms, H. K. Simon Co., Inc., 1280 Saw Mill River Rd, Yonkers, NY 10710.

Business Opportunities Digest, 301 Plymouth Drive, NE, Dalton, GA 30720

Executive Mart, 4 Tech Circle, Natick, MA 01760.

Sales and Marketing Exec-Cards, Hughes Communications, Inc., 11th floor, Rockford Trust Bldg., Rockford, IL 61101.

Salesman's Opportunity, Suite 1405, 6 N. Michigan Blvd, Chicago, IL 60602.

U.S. Sales & Marketing Briefs, Hughes Communications, Inc., 11th floor, Rockford Trust Bldg., Rockford, IL 61101.

NEWS-RELEASE DISTRIBUTION HELP

The following organization will distribute four hundred copies of your news release for you for a small fee:

Washington News Service
908 National Press Bldg.
Washington, DC 20045
202/737-4434

Index